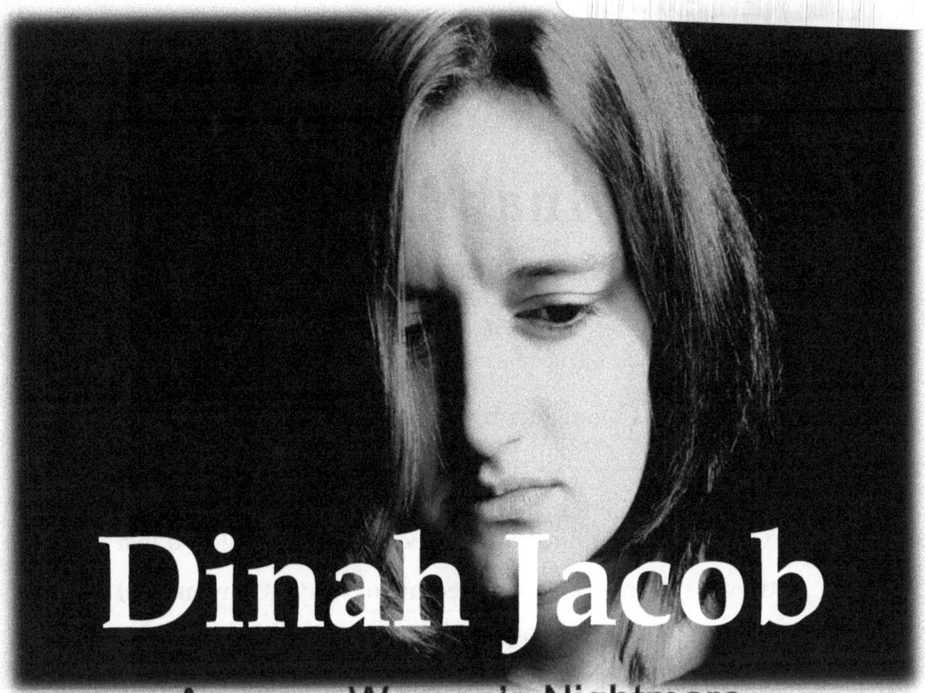

Dinah Jacob

A young Woman's Nightmare

On Her First Date

Silvanus Oluoch

Dinah Jacob
A young Woman's Nightmare
On Her First Date

Dinah Jacob © Silvanus 2018
All rights Reserved

No part of this publication may be reproduced, stored in a retrieval system, or transmitted in any way by any means, electronic, mechanical, photocopy, recording, or otherwise without the prior permission of the author, except as provided for by copyright laws.

ISBN: 9966-9991-1-6

Printed in the United States of America

Contacts: P O Box 69163, 00610 Nairobi, Kenya
E-mail: greatministries@yahoo.com

NOW DINAH daughter of Leah, whom she bore to Jacob, went out [unattended] to see the girls of the place. Genesis 34: 1 (AMP)

To all the young people who may not even realize they need necessary information on sex matters

Preface

This is a book that should be read by every young person who is serious about a wholesome love life. It does not tell the young people what they want to hear, but rather what they need to hear. In fact, even the cynics can learn a thing or two from it. It is impressively informative as it goes into details in describing what happened to Dinah, despite all that she had learned in life.

Its message is timeless, comprehensive and very much within the guidelines of the various disciplines; more so the mental health community. Seeking professional help, which the book advocates for is definitely the first step in securing healing from a traumatic experience. Yet more importantly is the step of becoming a part of a community of people with similar experiences, which the book recommends also. In such fora the victims learn, accept and support each other as part of their healing process.

This book not only talks of the healing process for traumatic experiences, but prudently outlines exploring God's components of love in the wisdom of a number of authors. It brings God into focus as the true healer. It also points to the limitations of human nature in expressing or desiring love in the examples of a number of case situations. Similarly, it touches on the liberal thinking (in sexual matters) that permeates our societies today.

I recommend it to every young person, who desires to be steadfast in the faith and seeks to steer clear of the youthful harbor of heartbreaks, occasioned by misinformation on sexual love.

      Esther Wanjihia
      Social worker, Seattle Washington   May 2013

Introduction

Dinah Jacob is a story of an ill-timed passion and betrayal involving a young woman whose family had just relocated into a new city. As soon as she picked-up friendships with the local girls and she began frequenting one of the girl's residence, a young man in the city got interested in her. Unfortunately, no one was prepared for what followed. Before they could even get well acquainted, the young man date-raped her on their first encounter to the dismay of everyone else.

It is a heart rending story that began well with the girl's birth, but did not end well. Because when the heinous act was perpetrated upon her, her brothers took the law into their own hands and slaughtered the whole city. Regrettably in this situation, the consequences were as harsh as was the act itself. Lamentably, this is not an isolated case. There are records showing that rape is a widespread and frequent phenomenon even today.

The thrust of this story is meant to alert the young people to the fact that rape and other sexual abuses are common and can happen to anyone. In fact, some studies have shown that at least a third of girls and a quarter of boys have been sexually molested or abused in some way. Young people, therefore, need to be well informed;

especially, on sexual matters so that they can avoid being victims. Such knowledge would also be instrumental in their being careful in choice of friends.

The Characters in this book are not related to anyone in real life. Some of them are my own creations, while others are biblical characters. I have taken the story of Dinah from the Bible's book of Genesis Chapter 34. I dramatized and expanded it, adding some fictitious characters so I could construct and present a lively story able to speak to the readers clearly.

In the beginning of the book, I am giving a little background to Dinah's family before I get to her personal story. I have written as if I favor the girl child simply because this story is about a girl and also because they are the most vulnerable to sexual manipulations in the name of love. The opinions and facts I have expressed herein are not all original with me; I have picked up some here and there along the way from a number of sources in my walk with God. But they are proven wisdom from a Judeo-Christian perspective based on the biblical principles, which are the best guide for every human life.

My intention in this book is to arouse the young people's curiosity to pursue relevant knowledge in this most important aspect of their lives. I did this because sometimes in matters of sex, some young people presume they are experts only to realize later that they were wrong. Right information is urgently needed today, because our social trends are leaning toward liberalism in everything including sex. Our young people are at crossroads; they need appropriate and accurate information to enable them safely weather the storms of current misinformation.

This little volume does not purport to be a textbook on sex or youth behavior, but it is a provocation to the young people to pursue relevant knowledge on sexology rightfully. Though it is small and does not exhaust all there is to be said on this subject; it is conservatively forthright and explicit in its address. If the young people can embrace and apply its message, they will be set free from trying to fit in with every convenient fad around them.

I have designed some thought provoking questions at the end of some of its chapters, which I consider very useful in leading discussions pertaining to the subject matter. They are to help stimulate open and frank discussions on life, sex and related issues. I believe they can be used in group settings, or even in personal study. This is the gist of the book where the succulent facts are buried. The discussions are suited to afford opportunities for the involved to contemporize the questions to their specific situations, or circumstances as may be applicable.

Although the book is small in volume, discussing the questions will definitely stretch its content. Some of the questions may require research into other available resources in the libraries and other resource centers. But overall, I trust this work will serve its purpose if it is read and applied.

The author

Acknowledgements

Julia Mariga did a fabulous work of going through the manuscript, correcting typos and other errors. In the process, she asked very relevant questions that helped me to restructure some of the sentences and chapters. For her contributions to the success of this work, I say thank you.

Rabbi Ted Simon, the Director of Planned Giving at the Salvation Army of Maryland, also took his precious time and read through the manuscript. He gave wonderful feedback and I am indebted to his insightful comments.

Eddie Khamlaundie with her friend Adwoa also read the manuscript, and they wondered how even, seemingly nice people can be that cruel! I give them a pat on the back for being such avid readers. To others who also contributed in one way or the other, but have decided to remain anonymous; I say grace and peace to you.

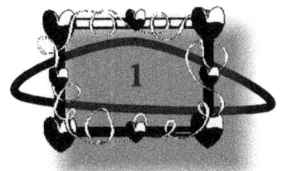

Dinah Enters the World

Dinah was Jacob's only known daughter from his wife Leah. She was born after a chain of six boys, and she must have come when even her mother had given up hopes of ever bearing a girl. The mother must have harbored that desire for a while, but after a series of boys it is probable she gave it up.

Then later on when she was not even interested in any more children, she happened to pick up a pregnancy and to the family's joy Dinah was born. The last of seven children from the same mother, she was the only girl. And being the last child born long after every one of her brothers, she was the teddy girl; mother's favorite child. Not only that but she was also everyone's favorite in the family.

When she was born the news about her birth spread around the city so quickly like wild fire. Then at the end of two years when she was weaned, a celebration was thrown on her behalf that brought many relatives and neighbors to their home. Her life was welcome with bright and serene sense of future greatness. Oh, what a bundle of joy and a source of unity she became at that very beginning of her life. This was at a time in her family when there were lots of strain and stresses involving much rivalry occasioned by the fact that her father had, in addition to her mother, married her aunt Rachel.

This resulted in a polygamous family with all its intrigues and squabbles. But Dinah's coming changed that for a while as love was expressed, not only to the baby girl but also to the mother. She grew up a fairly tender girl; a beauty with grace and dignity, somewhat taking after her mother yet having her father's deep greyish eyes. She was an assertive dark-haired young girl, who related quite well with all persons within and without her family.

She was talkative, but respectful and very sociable. Her family not only loved her, but they also cared deeply about her. She was pretty and charming, and it was everyone's expectation that she would grow up to be an instrument of change in the society at large; just like she brought change of atmosphere to her family at birth. Her brothers Simeon and Levi, especially had an exceptional love for her. Though much older than her, they usually allowed her to accompany them almost everywhere.

She continued to grow in that atmosphere of love and acceptance, displaying her own identity. She was adorable, especially to her family. In fact, as the only girl in the midst of boys; she grew up doing lots of 'boy' stuff. However, traditionally, the primary role of a woman she was to grow into was understood to be that of being a wife and a mother. Culturally there was great respect for the women and their importance as spiritual influencers of their families.

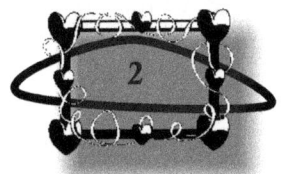

Sketches of Her Family Background

Dinah's dad as I mentioned earlier was called Jacob, who bore several children including this beautiful girl Dinah. Jacob's father was called Isaac, and he had two sons: Esau and Jacob himself.

As the two boys were growing up, one day Jacob got into a salient misunderstanding with his elder brother Esau. There was a standoff in Mr. Isaac's home. The younger son had defrauded his elder brother of his inheritance rights and the elder son was furious; he was planning to murder his brother. But then the mother who was acting as an adviser to the younger boy got wind of the scheme and asked him to leave home. That was the only sure way to keep him alive then. But where could he go, seeing that all his close relatives lived very far away!

However, the mother could not take any chances; she insisted the boy had to leave home at once, even if it would take him long to get to his uncle's place. Hence, she secretly organized and sent the younger boy off to his uncle who lived in a place called Padan-Aram.

From this we observe that as children grow up, sometimes there is usually what is referred to as sibling rivalry. Kids fight over toys, over rooms, or over who is more loved than the other and so forth. In Jacob's case their problem was about a birthright issue, which boiled down to being an inheritance matter. The situation got out of hand and Jacob had to flee his home and go stay with his uncle in a faraway place.

Jacob Goes to His Uncle

On arrival at his uncle's home in Haran, he was received well and he set himself for new beginnings. This place was slightly different from his home in Canaan as it was mainly a pastoralist country; although they were not nomads. People there had fixed abodes and practiced agriculture and animal husbandry. They kept large flocks of sheep and goats, herds of cows and oxen, domestic fowls and other animals. But having had his own flock back home, though on a smaller scale, his integrating into this large scale flock keeping could not take him long. He was a very flexible young man, ready to learn and adapt to whatever situations came by.

With this attitude it was not long before he freely accompanied his uncle's youngest daughter Rachel to the grazing fields. Rachel was charged with looking after her father's animals. Indeed, it was taken that the daughters were the dairy-maids. And it is for that reason that we meet Racheal out in the fields with animals. Of course, she was the first person of her family to meet Jacob when he first arrived in that city. It was that same Rachel who then took the news of Jacob's arrival to her family. Then the whole family warmly welcomed and gave him a free hand to be at home in their midst.

Shortly thereafter, he settled down with his heart set on service. Like I have mentioned, he began accompanying Rachel to the pastures to feed the animals. They were together all day on a daily basis and it did not take long before he realized he was in love with her. The love and fondness continued working itself between them as they spent days on end together herding the animals. Sometimes they chatted the whole time not even realizing how quickly time went by. Some other times Rachel had so many questions for Jacob about his home country. It is such conversations that kept their days going. The more they conversed, sharing and spending time together; the more they found themselves being drawn closer and closer to each other.

Then somehow an opportunity opened up for him to consider taking his relationship with Rachel, even further. This came about when one day his uncle summoned him for a private meeting. He did not know what it was all about at first; his heart pounded so fast when he imagined he might have offended unawares. But in the meeting his uncle quieted his apprehensions by informing him of how he had seen his dedication and hard work, in helping Rachel with the animals. His uncle was impressed with his love for, and devotion to his work. Therefore, the uncle was ready to pay for his services from then on. "Your services won't be free anymore," his uncle told him.

His uncle knew it was not right for people to work without some kind of payment. There would be no motivation if that continued so. That was a common teaching then and was even later proclaimed by one of their Hebrew prophets saying, "Woe unto him that builds his house by unrighteousness, and his chambers by wrong; that uses his neighbor's service without wages, and gives him not for his work."

Thus, Jacob's uncle gave him an option to determine what he needed for his payment. Then whatever it was they were to meet again and agree on it to make sure all sides were satisfied. But Jacob did not wait for another day. There and then he openly declared his love for Rachel telling his uncle he would take her for his payment.

Somehow the uncle was astonished at the young man's proposal, but he did not show it openly. He never expected such an answer and that quick. But since he had given the young man a free hand in making a choice, he somewhat accepted his nephew's request. But in his mind, he was yet to reconcile himself with it. He needed to figure out how to go around that agreement as it was unworkable; definitely, impossible in their cultural set-up. He could not give away the younger daughter in marriage before her elder sister.

In Rachel's case, her elder sister Leah was not yet married and culturally there was no way she could be given in marriage without having Leah married off first. Jacob's request put the uncle in a difficult situation, but his uncle did not mention it. Anyway it was something they would face as it developed further, or the boy would develop other interests; so the uncle thought. He did not want to dishearten his young nephew by plainly telling him his request could not be honored. With that issue suspended in their minds, Jacob got down to business.

Time passed quickly as Jacob continued with his work, while at the same time growing much closer to Rachel. Finally, time was fulfilled as per his agreement with his uncle and then he asked for his Rachel. Still caught off guard, his uncle must have consulted the townsmen on how to proceed.

Based on their advice he then planned for the wedding to go on as scheduled. Every arrangement was made and invitations sent far and wide. Bridal preparation was also put in top gear as per their customs and traditions. In that process the uncle managed to disguise

Leah the eldest daughter and gave her over to Jacob in marriage as Rachel.

Come the following morning Jacob realized he had been duped. On discovering what was done to him, Jacob did not feel good about it. "How can my uncle who portrayed himself as an understanding and a reasonable loving person do such a thing to me? Why did he not just tell me plainly that my request could not be honored instead of beguiling me?" he wondered aloud.

But there was a principle at work in that whole process. Jacob was somehow reaping the fruits of what he himself had done earlier on when he took Esau's blessings. You know he had disguised himself, impersonating Esau and he cheated his old father out of Esau's blessings. By then his father was very old and blind and he took advantage of that to cheat him.

His father had intended to "bless" Esau by conferring the right of being the elder son upon him as were their customs. But Jacob got the wind of this and disguised himself as Esau and deceived his father. He took that right although he knew he was not the first born. Although greatly suspicious, the father blessed him anyway only to realize he had been cheated when Esau finally came home. And that is what brought about the misunderstanding, which led to Jacob's flight to his uncle.

So there at his uncle's he was subjected to the same thing he had done to his brother. He had shortchanged his brother and now he also stood shortchanged. Sometimes the things we do to others will be done to us by others. The good Book unequivocally states that don't be misled: No one makes a fool of God. What a person plants, he will harvest. The person, who plants selfishness, ignoring the needs of others, ignoring God, will himself reap exactly what he has planted. He will be ignored in time.

This means, if we treat people with respect and love; we will also be treated the same way one time or another. But if we are rude and mean to others; we must realize we will definitely meet those same types of attitudes. However, the best treatment we should accord people is respect; respecting them as individuals and even their properties.

Anyway after being tricked into marrying the woman he did not choose, Jacob did not give up on his love for Rachel whom he had grown fond of. He loved her so much to let her go. He could not bring himself to live without her. In fact, they had spent so much time together and their love for each other had grown tremendously. He needed her and he was ready to do anything to get her. He believed there was a way of getting her. Hence, he went to talk to his uncle about it.

His uncle might have thought he would be satisfied with just any woman and hence gave him Leah. But the uncle was wrong, the Jacob-Rachel love could not just end that easily. There was still a strong longing in Jacob's heart for her. So he raised his complaints with his uncle, who seeing his nephew's determination entered into another seven years contract with him concerning Rachel.

In the process of time, Leah began to bear children. In fact, she bore Jacob six sons and finally a daughter they named Dinah, whose story we are recounting on the pages that follow.

Some Questions to Ponder

1. As Dinah's story begins we find ourselves talking about her family: father and other relatives. What is significant about this?
2. Everybody is or should be connected to (others) a family somewhere somehow; it may be a biological or even adoptive family, or even just friends but nonetheless a family of sorts. Families play important roles in our lives, do you agree or disagree? Discuss giving reasons.
3. There is a saying that what you do to others will be done to you one time or another; how true is it and

what does this teach us? Is it the so-called cause and effects?
4. When Jacob arrived at his uncle's place he had an attitude that made things slightly easy for him in his early days there. What was it, and why is it important in life? Explain
5. The normal assumption in life is that everyone is unique, but sometimes people say things like all (men) boys are the same; or that all (women) girls are the same. Is this true or not? Discuss in what sense they are the same or different.
6. What was unique about Dinah? What is unique about you as a person?
7. We have read that Dinah was an inspiration to her family; what are the indications of this? How can we also be inspirational to our families or be of any positive impact? Can we know if we are impactful at all? Explain.

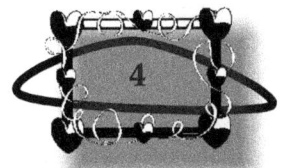

Jacob at Loggerheads With His Uncle

In the cause of time after he had fulfilled his second seven years contract and eventually married Rachael; a difficult situation arose between Jacob and his uncle's family. It was so bad that while serving his uncle, he reached a point in life where he wanted to quit. He felt that his uncle was playing tricks on him and misusing him. This forced him to secretly plan to relocate to Canaan. As you must be aware, he had come to his uncle to escape his brother's wrath. Yet by then much time had elapsed and feelings had changed too. He hoped things were not as bad as they had been in the heat of the moment of his deception.

In those early years he had come to his uncle alone as a young man, but now after the elapse of many years; he was a family man with many children. Logically, his whole family if he was to relocate was to do so with him.

Without wasting time he said to his uncle, "Release me from our agreement and let me return to my own country, I have worked, serving you very well; it is time I took my wives and children and left."

But his uncle replied, "Permit me to tell you not to go yet, I know God has blessed me because of you. I still need God's blessings through you; just let me know what your pay should be this time and I will give it to you."

However, Jacob declined to name any specific wage package; rather he entered into an agreement concerning types of animals. But that very day his uncle took away all the male animals; the types Jacob had mentioned in his contract. When he saw that Jacob sensed that his uncle was not serious, he was only playing tricks on him.

Like someone said, it was evident that the blessing of God was upon him, and everything he did prospered. Hence, old Laban wanted to keep him around for personal gain. But then Jacob devised a plan to counter-trick his uncle, which he did and he ended up with the strongest and most animals. He became very rich in flocks and herds of animals at the expense of his uncle.

Then one day he overheard his cousins (Laban's sons) talking among themselves how he (Jacob) came to their home empty handed, but had by then become very rich. They claimed he had acquired so much possessions from their father's wealth to enrich himself. He learned that they were grumbling about him saying, "Jacob has robbed our father of everything! He has gained all his wealth at our father's expense."

In other words, he had interfered with their inheritance. It looked like he was always bent on interfering with people's inheritances. First it was his brother's and then it was his cousins'. But they vowed never to let that happen in their case. They were not going to take it lying down. Something had to be done to Jacob to stop him from taking any more of their father's wealth. It had to be done soonest and they were ready to do it.

After that conversation among themselves, they developed hard feelings toward Jacob. He noticed that they had indeed become cold and indifferent (unfriendly) to him. Indeed, even his uncle Laban's attitude too changed. But he was more worried about the young men whom he believed must have been plotting some kind of mischief than he was his uncle. His only best option then was to leave Haran as soon as possible and go reconcile with his brother Esau whom he had defrauded earlier on.

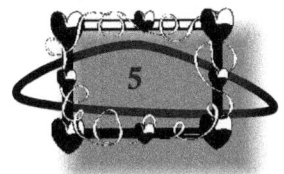

Relocation and Its Effects

Jacob told his wives about this developing situation and his immediate intentions, and they were very supportive and positive in their responses. Rachel and Leah responded, "That's fine with us! We won't inherit any of our father's wealth anyway. He has reduced our rights to those of foreign women. And after he sold us, he wasted the money you paid him for us. All the wealth God has given you from our father legally belongs to us and our children. So go ahead and do whatever God has told you."

With such an assurance and cooperation from his wives; Jacob was determined to make good his intentions. The only lingering uncertainty was the children's response. All of his children had been born in Haran and did not consider anywhere else as home. All they knew was Haran and when their father mentioned that they had to leave and go 'home'; they had so many unanswered questions. But there was no time to make them understand. There was no two way about it; the situation was grave and was getting worse by the day.

Thus, their family had to relocate to Canaan their father's birthplace. They were to leave all their friends and acquaintances and go begin life a fresh. It was an intimidating thought at first, but having no otherwise; they consented. So Jacob took his wives and children and driving his livestock in front of him; he began the long journey back home to the land of Canaan where his father lived. He carried everything, which he had acquired while in Haran. This he did while his uncle had gone away to sheer his sheep some distance from Haran.

Finally they arrived safely to the new city, which was a country-city type of place. On their arrival they were overwhelmingly welcome by its residents coming out in large numbers to receive them into their midst. Eventually, Jacob bought a part of the field from the descendants of that city's mayor Mr. Hamor, the father of Shechem, for a hundred pieces of silver. There, slightly off the city-center, he set his camp and established his family in the neighborhood which he called Shelters within the city of Shechem in the country of Canaan.

Lifestyle and culture in this new place was totally alien to what they were used to in Haran. It was totally different, everything from culture to the dialect was dissimilar. The atmosphere too seemed freer here than in

Haran. Jacob's children especially Dinah had some difficulties at first, for in Haran girls rarely went out except in the company of relatives or in a group. But in this new city even girls roamed the streets freely with no watchful eyes on them.

Nonetheless, Dinah soon adapted quite well to life in this new place. Soon, the biblical records recount that NOW DINAH daughter of Leah, whom she bore to Jacob, went out [unattended] to see the girls of the place. This new city provided her an opportunity to freely involve and interact with other girls without having to be accompanied by her brothers. Having grown most of her life among her brothers; this new atmosphere was kind of intimidating at first.

However, she quickly made friends with various girls in the new city. Tina a lovely young girl, who looked much older for her age, became her best friend. Tina lived with her mother, who usually left chores for her to do during the day. The mother generally returned home much later in the evening from their family business of selling groceries and grains. Her dad had passed away earlier on in life when she was only a baby, and so it was just Tina and her mother.

Enquiry Made About Dinah

Dinah somehow developed a liking for Tina and frequented her residence. In one of such visits, her fair tenderness caught the eyes of a young man known as Shechem, who had a namesake with the city. He then came to Tina's residence one mid-morning enquiring about Dinah. His conversation with Tina went something like this:

"Good morning Tina; how are you doing today?" asked Shechem.

"Oh, I am fine sir. Where are you off to this early?" responded Tina.

"Mmm, I am just around; it is you I wanted to see. Do you have a minute I need to ask you something?" Shechem added.

"Sure, what's up?" Tina asked.

"The other day I saw you with a girl here I have never seen around this neighborhood. Who is she and where is she?" Shechem asked.

"Ooh, that is Dinah Jacob one of my new friends; they just moved into town recently from Padan-Aram," answered Tina

"You mean to tell me she is the daughter of that rich guy who purchased our piece of property a few months ago?" further enquired Shechem.

"Yes she is," answered Tina.

"Is she approachable?"

"Yeah, she is very friendly and outgoing," chipped in Tina.

"I would love to meet her. When do you expect to see her again?" enquired Shechem.

"She will be coming here any time, but especially this afternoon." Intimated Tina.

"All right, pass me a word whenever she comes by; it would be great for me to meet her too." Shechem said enthusiastically.

"Take care, I hope to see you later. Have a nice day." Shechem added as he walked away.

Tina inwardly wondered what interest Shechem had in the new girl, who had just moved to their city recently. Personally, she grew up there in Canaan and Shechem had never approached her in any way but casual. In fact, She had admired him secretly for a while desiring a relationship with him. Yet he never even approached her and that desire kept burning within her all that time. Like other young women, she did not make any move to let him know. She was afraid as she did not know how he might have reacted.

Indeed, she obsessed over him for a while, but that was as far as that obsession went. It was common in those days, and even today for young women to wait for boys or men to make the first move. Although that is currently changing with the advent of modern communication technologies.

Nonetheless, when Shechem came knocking at their gate that mid-morning Tina was both elated and surprised at the same time. She was not prepared for him and did not know even what to tell him. However, it turned out that his visit was not about her. Anyway she adopted a wait-and-see attitude.

By the way, Shechem was not just another guy in town; he was named after that very city's name. He was the son of the city's prince, who happened to be its mayor. That meant any sensible girl or woman desirous of high status in that society would have definitely spoken nicely to him. Is it any wonder then that for some times even

Tina had secretly admired him? But he seemed not to realize Tina's admiration. Or did he ignore her as a girl he saw growing up?

Some Questions to Ponder

1. How was life going for Dinah's dad at his uncle's? Discuss.
2. Why did Jacob's children struggle with the relocation idea at first?
3. What would have been your reaction, if were you one of Jacob's children?

Dinah Goes to Her Friend's Residence

The midmorning clouds had just cleared and the sun shone through in the sky giving an indication of a warm afternoon to follow. Dinah was at home going through her chores. She helped with the baking of loaves of bread, cutting some cucumbers and preparing olives and cheese; all to be used at dinner time. When she was done, she took a quick shower and dressed up in a grayish cotton skirt and a bluish blouse. Nonetheless, she did not put on her traditional flowing gown that covered the whole body.

Since they moved into this new city she had been in the habit of dressing up just like the town's girls, unlike where she came from where even the girls' choice of wardrobe (clothing) was controlled. Here, she was beginning to be a bit freer. She then brushed her long black hair, which she had done up in a bun and made it into a long braid down her back. She was then ready, and off she went to her friend Tina's residence.

Tina had been waiting for her ever since Shechem came enquiring about her that morning. Even though Dinah herself did not know what to expect that day; she somehow felt like there was a new challenge awaiting her. On arrival at her friend's residence Tina greeted her enthusiastically saying,

"Good afternoon Dinah, how are you dear? I am excited to see you. Can I offer you something to drink it is quite hot today?"

"Yeah, it is hot but I am fine if you do not mind; thank you," replied Dinah politely. Then she added, "It seems to me to be a good day though, do you feel the same or is it just me?"

"Of course it is a good day," agreed Tina. Then she added, "For your information some guy was here in the morning asking for you."

"Some guy was here enquiring about me, did he think I live here?" Asked Dinah inquisitively.

"No! I think it is simply because he saw you here," Tina responded.

"Who is he and what did he want?" Dinah asked surprised.

"He is called Shechem; I don't know if you have met him yet?" Tina responded.

"You definitely know I have not met anyone like that; I am new in this place." Dinah said.

"What exactly was he asking?" She further enquired.

"Just general things like who you are and so forth," answered Tina

"And what did you tell him?" Dinah probed.

"Nothing much, I just mentioned that you are new in town." Tina explained.

"What sort of a guy is he; tall, short . . . ?" asked Dinah.

"He is medium built with somewhat a short round face, but you will see him for yourself I cannot describe him properly; I am poor at describing people." Tina answered.

"You mean he is still around!" Enquired Dinah astonishingly.

"No; he is not here at the moment, but he is from around and he promised to pass-by later on. I have a hunch he is interested in you," explained Tina.

Dinah gave her a disapproving look and objected saying, "I do not even know him how can you claim he is interested in me?"

"Don't give me that look my dear. May be, or maybe not." Tina responded.

"What do you mean may be, or maybe not? Does that mean he may be interested and not interested in me at the same time?" Dinah interjected.

"I do not care about him and I would not give him an audience even if he were here now." She added.

"My dear I am not suggesting you give him an audience, or that you hook up with him. I am simply expressing my feelings based on his enquiry." Tina clarified.

"But I am not interested in him, or in any man for that matter. I don't come here looking for men, and I do not want anything to do with this man you are telling me about." Dinah expressed firmly.

"Why not?" Enquired Tina.

"Simply because I do not know him, and I do not see how he can claim to be interested in me. I am not that sort of a person, you know. Furthermore, I am only here for our friendship." Dinah responded.

"Oh, Dinah do not say that. Shechem is loaded; he is the mayor's son. You should consider yourself lucky that he is interested in you." Chipped in Tina.

"I have told you I am not interested in him; can we discuss something else?" Dinah responded.

But Tina went on to bring Dinah up to speed on Shechem's identity as one of the most important people in that community. However, Dinah was not interested. She finally interjected saying,

"I do not care the least how rich or poor a guy is. It is who they are that should really matter."

"That is what I am trying to do, letting you know exactly who this guy Shechem is." Tina responded.

"Hold it. I have told you I am not interested in that guy." Dinah said kind of wanting to change the subject. But then Tina added,

"Shechem is kind of handsome."

"So what if he is? Let's leave him alone. Do you have anything I can help you with today?" Dinah finally asked in a bid to change the topic.

The girls then engaged in some non-personal conversations while Dinah helped Tina out with some of her chores. Tina's mom often left her chores only to return home much later in the evening from their family business. Meanwhile Tina secretly sent a word to Shechem that Dinah had arrived at her residence.

But then how was Dinah to respond to this young man, who was showing strong interests in her? It is reported that he fell in love with her, and wanted to win her affection with tender words. Unfortunately, Dinah was ill prepared for this attraction. First, she presumed that everyone held her kind of values. Yet, clearly people don't all hold or subscribe to same values, especially if they are from different cultural backgrounds. And even within the same cultures people still have different orientations and convictions.

Dinah was ill prepared for this attraction also, because her relationship with her brothers had conditioned her differently. She presupposed that young men were as respectful as were her brothers; or that they love and care for girls, just for who they are. But she was soon to find out that that was a misconception. Some boys or even men only love girls for what they can get from them! They really do not love the girls, but what the girls have. The girls as their source of pleasures to be enjoyed on demand! That seemed to have been the culture in that city of Shechem.

Contemporarily, such attractions are common, mostly referred to as a *crush*. Sometimes it even occurs among some very, very young people. However, such an attraction if not guided properly can end up in heartaches that may alter those young people's lives forever in terms of relationships. That is one of the reasons young people are cautioned to get to know people first before committing to anything. They must choose their friends wisely, discerning if their values are compatible. Values involving affiliations: religious or otherwise, social leanings and so forth. Even the good Book affirms that choosing friends carefully is wise, whereas the decisions of the unstable leads them astray.

The young man Shechem, finally arrived at Tina's residence in response to Tina's message. Tina then went ahead and introduced them saying,

"Dinah; this is Shechem, the guy I mentioned had come asking for you. And Shechem this is Dinah Jacob my friend."

"My pleasure to meet you Ms. Jacob," Shechem said extending his hand to greet Dinah.

Dinah graciously took his hand saying, "Thanks; it is my pleasure too." Then she added, "Please call me Dinah."

"Thanks Ms. Dinah, I kindly take note of that." Shechem said looking her in the eyes.

They then engaged in a brief chit-chat, after which Shechem excused himself requesting to leave. However he wanted to leave with Dinah so as to go show her around the city as they got acquainted further. He offered to take her for a walk across the city's Gateway Park; the monumental place in Shechem. With that he intended to spend some time alone with her conversing and getting to know her better. At first Dinah was hesitant feeling uneasy about it, but Tina convinced her saying it was all right. She informed her not to fear Shechem, as he was a gentleman.

In fact, Tina thought he was interesting and safe to be around. She told Dinah how outgoing and loquacious he was, hinting that she would not be bored if she went with him.

"Is he really a good guy?" Dinah had asked her privately seeking for some assurance.

"You'll be fine," Tina assured her. Then added, "To the best of my knowledge he is good, but the best way to really find out is to take his challenge and go out with him."

Finally, Dinah accepted the offer and left with Shechem promising to pass by shortly on her way home. Shechem was elated as he walked away with Dinah besides him; whereas to Dinah this was one of her major moves in this new city. She had never gone out one on one with a fellow like Shechem.

As a young energetic girl out to fully explore her new environment at leisure, she did not anticipate any troubles; either to herself, or to anyone else. Yet like most young people, she had the bent to live for her friend's approval; peer pressure was at work in her life too. As a known fact, young people are always influenced in one way or the other by their peers and other factors. Dinah was no exception. She had been influenced a lot by Tina and others.

For instance, when Tina told her about Shechem; she did not want to appear naïve, especially on matters of boy-girl relationships. But did she really know how to handle folks like Shechem? And who was this Shechem by the way? That is what we want to find out in our next chapter. However, before then let's review.

Some Questions to Ponder

1. We read that before Dinah left home she engaged in some house chores that were definitely part of her responsibility. What does this tell us about her? Why is being a responsible young person right from home important?

2. What were some of Dinah's strong personal traits? Are you aware of what your strong personal traits are?
3. How does Dinah generally differ from young girls today and from you as a young person?
4. Dinah obviously did some things out of peer pressure; what is peer pressure?
5. How are you as a young person to handle or face such pressures?
6. Can you remember an occasion when you succumbed to peer pressures, may be you were forced to smoke a cigarette or did something you would not have done otherwise? How did you feel or dealt with the situation afterwards?

A Glimpse into Shechem's Background

As we have already observed, Shechem was the son of the city's ruler. He grew up a privileged child who presumed that he had a right to everything he wanted. But he lacked morals, principles and decency. There had been many occasions when he rubbed some of the community members the wrong way, and the reports of such incidences never failed to reach his dad. But whatever advice his dad gave him were never made public.

Nonetheless, he was not a stranger to controversies. In fact, he was known for his escapades with young women around the city. Based on who he was; it is probable that even some of the young women sought him out, though that was not the case with Dinah.

Before his encounter with Dinah, he had had another tumultuous love relationship with Luhtar Muhti;

a young woman who came to live with her aunt in Shechem sometimes back. Luhtar's aunt was a very protective guardian who took the girl after her family was killed in an inter-clan feud miles away from Shechem. Relatives went and took the survivors after the place was razed to the ground on an attack, occasioned by quarrels over grazing fields and watering points.

    Muhti was fortunate enough to have had an aunt and an uncle who cared enough to take her in. She braced herself and adapted to life in Shechem city very quickly and soon forgot her past. Then in no time she grew up to be a gorgeously beautiful young woman and Shechem made a move for her. He followed her everywhere, even to the water wells and to the market and often took her to his home. Sometimes she never even did her house chores, especially when she went with Shechem.

    Her aunt was disappointed at the turn of events and spoke to the young woman on several occasions. She expressed her displeasure at Muhti's involvements with the young man, Shechem. She gave her many reasons why she needed to stop her involvement with him, but she could not listen. Despite her aunt's pleas of disapproval and protestations; she refused to break her involvements with him. By then she had developed very strong emotional ties to the guy.

It looked like her life had totally changed by her involvement with him. In fact, she experienced a behavioral change that turned her into a rude girl, especially towards her aunt.

"Shechem is my love; he cherishes me so much, and I do not want to hurt his feelings. I cannot leave him, and nothing will separate us." She once told her aunt.

By then she was exhibiting some of the worst attitudes toward her aunt almost in everything. She claimed that Shechem was her life and all she ever needed; he understood her and made her comfortable. She further expressed that she could not live without him, and vowed never to be separated from him

When her aunt failed to prevail upon her, the aunt then confronted the young man demanding he stopped exploiting Luhtar. But the young man with I-don't-care attitude denied exploiting the girl. He claimed to love her very much. That case then turned into a big issue that was finally taken to the city gates for the elders to deliberate on. That move brought much focus and attention on Shechem as his love affair with Luhtar became the whole city's issue. Somehow, because of his family's influence; Luhtar's aunt and family were coerced to relocate from Shechem city and they did so reluctantly.

Unawares of that background, Dinah thought being friends with such a fellow was just like being friends with her brothers. That was the only relationship she knew well enough to gauge others with. Nonetheless, she loved friendships as in them she looked for opportunities to develop her relational skills. Yet, on this occasion she displayed a naivety not common in Canaan and Shechem, who claimed to love her found an opportunity to exploit.

Some Questions to Ponder

1. When Tina assured Dinah that Shechem was a good man, did she trick her friend or did she really know Shechem?
2. What does your answer to the above question teach us?
3. Do you think Shechem exploited Luhtar or theirs was a mutual friendship and the auntie was just being sensitive for nothing? Expalin
4. What made the girl think that Shechem really loved her?

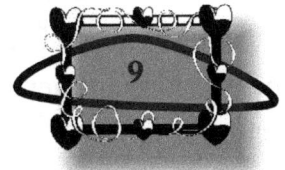

Wisdom from Padan-Aram

We have seen that Shechem, a young man had just expressed some strong interests in Dinah. Whereas she had come from a culture where young people never freely showed open interest in others like that. Free relationships between boys and girls were not allowed or encouraged. Rather such relationships were strongly controlled; mostly to prevent sexual involvements. Young people's relationships and lives reflected on and affected their families' status in the wider society. Hence, they were tightly controlled to prevent their engagements in things that would reflect negatively on their families.

They did not have individualistic notions of personal freedom in matters relational or even love. Life was approached from a communal perspective. Such young people were socialized to think in terms of the tribe and the clan. Especially, the girls were greatly restricted and not allowed to express their feelings or follow their hearts freely. They were shielded as the families' treasures.

That was the kind of culture Dinah came from; where strict cultural codes of conduct with specific values of rights and wrongs were enforced. These were inculcated in them as young people to help them grow up with the ideas of responsible citizenship.

They were deeply coached on family's private and public prayers; domestic rites and festive activities, and all the traditional wisdom of the land. It was impressed upon them that if they were to be worthwhile and unfettered in life; they were to live devoted to principles of purity and truth. They were to remember that without a virtuous moral basis even the best of experiences were but passing clouds.

The processing of such values was hoped would help them acquire the sense of worth and responsibility, or so it was thought. Concern for reputation and integrity was deeply etched into their minds through such tutorage. They were made aware of the fact that they would not remain children forever. They had to learn to grow up into responsible adults. Her society understood that young people must appropriately learn early enough in order to be worthy citizens.

Thus, their tutelage begun as early as five years of age or thereabout. They were trained in such ways that were considered true wisdom in the fear of Yahweh. Such trainings involved, but not limited to matters of personal conduct in the society or what was also called the rules for social life.

As already pointed out they were taught things like duty to one's society, and to oneself; they were taught self-respect and peer respect; respect for people's property, and respect for the elderly. Then there was the respect for authority, and defense of or protection of women and children. Not left behind were the values of, and care for animals; the meaning and value of work, the nature and importance of sex and marriage and other relevant things. Last but not least, they were impressed with the mysteries of Yahweh's religion; always reminded that they were a special people of the covenant.

Especially, the girls were impressed with the ideas that they were daughters of the highest "King"; referring to God. This was to enable them carry themselves with highest dignity that royalty deserves. They were not to carry themselves just as some common or ordinary people; they were not ordinary. They needed to realize and maintain that they were special. That was very important in giving them an elevated worldview of themselves. The trainings would not have been complete if they were not taught family traditions enshrined on cultural and religious values.

They instilled in them the necessary values of truthfulness, accountability and discipline; all expected to result in responsible citizenry. The goal, as I have stated, was to help them become honorable and responsible people in that society; largely held together by their beliefs, and devotion to Yahweh. But these values Dinah found lacking in most of the young people in Canaan; no one seemed to care much about what others, including kids did.

In Canaan the society seemed to be very permissive and indifferent to value-living. The people did not seem to care about moral or ethical values. Moreover, the young women did not seem to have been taught any principles of virtuous womanhood. This was unlike Haran where the girls were socialized and prepared to later meet the demands of their responsibilities as integrate female members of the society. And such young women grew up to be champions of family values that kept their society going without the general social erosions common then.

They were cultured to find their true identity and worth, involving acceptance at home first. This was done by being closely watched, helped and controlled to prevent their involving in sex outside marriage. The daughter's virginity was a matter of great concern, especially on the wedding night. It was held as a sign of integrity, honor and dignity even for the girl's family. Those families that wanted to maintain their pride and good standing in the society, fearing being let down on that wedding night, encouraged their daughters to remain virgins. To remain a virgin was a great honor for the girl's family.

They held that the daughter reflected the mother, as went a common saying *like mother like daughter*. A loose girl running around with boys or men was not good news to any respectable family. Such a girl was considered a disgrace and a source of shame, disrespect and a nuisance to her family in their closely knit society.

Nonetheless, sex was a big issue then even as it is today; except that for them it was a resolved issue. This was in the sense that it was not considered something to be exploited, simply for personal pleasures as is the case today. The society was not as individualistic as ours has become. Yet, some parents then even as today; did not, or were unwilling to address it. They found it somewhat embarrassing.

However, those with strong religious convictions like Dinah's family considered sex a valuable endowment by the creator. To them it contained the highest potential for comradeship, spirituality and a means of expressing holy living in marriage. Their traditions taught them that marriage was the bonding link for the spiritual, emotional and even physical wellbeing of a husband and his wife. Hence, sex was to be preserved for marriage. It was not to be taken casually or regarded lightly, because it could make or break lives. They conceived it as the great cohesive force that pulls and binds the couples together, and continues the race as the link between the generations.

Thus, they were taught that casual sex was to be avoided; it was a mere momentary gratification that did not fulfill the real inner longings of the individuals. In most cases, it ended up building anxiety and other negative emotions in the involved individuals instead.

They were taught that it demeaned the value of worthwhile personhood, by destroying the bonds of deep meaningful and lasting relationships. It eroded (took away) that deep connection that arises from true intimate union of hearts. Casual sex is built on the misconceptions that sexual involvement is all that people need in life. More so, as a thrilling participation and an outlet for their steamed up emotions. Some people then, even as now, believed such a myth and ended in reckless sexual behaviors searching for the happiness that never is.

Nonetheless, in Padan-Aram they (the youth) were taught to abstain from such matters for their protection from the emotional pains and hurts that result from undertaking them prematurely. One of their Sages had put it that such prohibitions were for their protection and later timely and perfect provisions. They learned that sexual activities carry with them unannounced moral responsibilities, and hidden psychological consequences. Disregarding such wisdom always often lead to a sense of loss, loneliness and alienation, guilt and worthlessness, self-doubt and heartaches untold. Sadly, that which is considered a pleasurable experience turns around and hurts the people involved in it.

It was made clear to them that the notion of free-love or free-sex is a myth; it was a misguided passion people referred to as free-love. Clearly, there was nothing free about *free-sex*. The involved individuals have to pay the cost or the consequences somehow, even if not immediate. Because sure enough, as the sun rises from the east; the consequences would definitely arise from such involvements. Sadly, some youths never cared that there would be consequences to their actions whether undertaken in secrecy or not.

Accordingly, they were taught that sexual intercourse was not just a simple act of pleasure. It is a complex interaction that involves another person's whole being, including their fears and complexes. That is, although there is the physical aspect to sexual involvements; it also carries deep relational, emotional and even spiritual dimensions.

The relational aspect, more so the nature of the relationship, determines culpability of the whole involvement. Yet, a real wonderful sexual intimacy demands a secure environment in a committed ongoing relationship that only marriage could afford.

They were told that it does not matter how much (young) people may feel they love each other; sex was not for them before marriage. Sex outside marriage does not build or increase love. The opposite is the case, it destroys love by exposing one to unending fleshly lusts and unsavory stressful emotions. It is the casting of one's life on the hedonistic platform, estimating and hoping all will be well that is not well. They learnt that as wonderful as sex is, it can be problematic dependence on how it is approached and handled.

That is the reason sex at the wrong time, in a relationship not designed for it often results in emotional and psychological problems. It rarely affords opportunities for accountability and meaningful development of intimacy that make relationships fun. In other words, there is no accountability in loosely held involvements. It turns the pleasures and glory of sex into a self-serving exercise that then internally generates guilt in the minds of the involved. A phenomenon meant to be a source of joy and undying commitment to one another, turns into a source of pain, anxiety and dread. It casts away the very spring and bond of mutual intimacy that deep friendship is.

All that was based on the approach and perceptions men and women brought to sex. They learned that both sexes had different outlooks on sex. They were told that to most men, sex is just something they do and get over with. Whereas to a woman, sex is giving; the giving of herself, her emotions (of love and fears), and her heart all wrapped up in that act. In giving herself the woman is "trusting" that the receiving man will cherish and esteem her treasures above any other.

In other words, she longs to belong to him; she is ready to be possessed and obsessed about. She looks forward to being accepted, possessed and appreciated by him as the one and only. By that she casts her lot of belonging and best friendship with him, trusting he will solely be hers as she is ready to be his. That is the reason every woman wants a concrete assurance in matters related to love and sexual involvements. They will look you in the eye and wonder if you are really true and committed to their desires of wanting to belong to you. Without this, jealousies and other emotional insecurities often flare up in such relationships.

Basically, sexual love was designed to signify God's pure and fulfilling love. Yet the sexual love is satisfying only when encapsulated in a deeply personal and exclusive relationship built on trust that can never be found in a quick one time involvement. Neither can it be found even if the involvement is repeated, because of the very nature of such open involvements. They are non-committal, and are open to several and different abuses.

Moreover, it has been stated that a woman's sexual desires focus mostly on (one) a specific individual to ratify it by passionate love, coached in mutual agreement of trust and respect. That is the reason when a man decides to run off with other women, it is always devastating and heart-rending to his woman. Her trust and high hopes are crushed at the man's whims. Yet it does not seem to bother the man. It is then that her feminine relational self-preservative instinct of *positive jealousy,* kicks in immediately as a means of protecting what she values most and knows to belong to her. Not that she is a bad woman, but that is just the natural or normal reaction to anything that threatens her relationship.

Whereas to the man; sex is just something he does or engages in with these other women for fun, to make him feel great. It is mostly about him and his feelings. No wonder, it has been suggested that that is the reason the women who tell men "I can make you happy" often win them quite easily. Seemingly, men are mostly after happiness derivable from such women.

On the other hand, women are looking for more than just happiness; they are looking for security and privilege of belonging to a trustworthy, loving and caring man. When such a man sincerely loves and cares for his woman, it empowers and encourages her to contribute to their personal experiential development together; geared towards authentic being. That is, it gives her an emotional boost and connection that opens her up, broadening her capacity to love and be loved. This is all because generally the women's nature is positively possessive, and so is their need to be possessed so they can possess the possessor.

Wisdom from Padan-Aram Continued

Those young people were taught that personal discipline and self-control were a must for every young people, who wanted to engage another in a relationship that may eventually result in long-term marriage. Before they became husband and wife; they were taught to keep themselves pure from sexual promiscuity, if their relationship was to flourish and be enjoyably long lasting. They were not supposed to play around with the sacred gifts of sex that God had endowed them with.

One translation of the Holy book put it thus: "Therefore remove (the lust that ends in) sorrow and vexation from your heart and mind and put away evil from your body, for youth and the dawn of life are vanity and transitory, idle, empty and devoid of truth."

Many of them were surprised to learn from God's word that His standard prohibits premarital, free-sex or open sexual involvements. These are exploitative acts that do not portray His love. Such acts result in loss of self-respect and are a violation of God's moral law. Hence, these young people were taught to exercise self-control as their learnt to wait in such matters. They were reminded they would later appreciate that they waited in matters of sex, which is mostly worthwhile in marriage.

Any young people desiring to mount up to greater heights of social and marital blessings in their future, must surrender to Yahweh's guidelines for living in their present times. Their lives, whether private or public must be highly honorable and deeply pious. They must shun acts, which easily arouse strong sexual desires before the proper time. If not shunned, such acts would frustrate their relationships and create difficulties in their progress towards meaningful marriages. They were informed that a number of such relationships break up even before they take-off, leaving the involved young people with emotional scars and hurts.

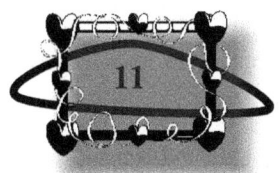

What Use Is Friendship?

In her relationships with Tina and others within that city, Dinah had begun learning new ways of responding to various situations and adapting to her new environment. It was her way of finding her balance. Since she had been going out with these Canaanite girls; they had all tended to talk more about boyfriends, love and boy related stuff. Yet, from her upbringing she had been taught that relationships; especially, friendships are good only if they are mutual and non-exploitative where one person uses the other. They had been told that if someone truly loves another, they would not choose to exploit them in the name of love. Because true love never exploits others. It desires the best for everyone involved in it rather than take advantage of them to gratify personal lusts. Unfortunately, in Canaan that was not the case.

Friendships there seemed to be about trying to use your friends as much as you could. Friendship were only about individual or personal advantage whatever that was! Then there were those who always wanted to dominate and control friendships at the expense of the others, especially the girls. But those Canaanite girls did not seem to see any problem with that.

Nonetheless, the young women were cautioned to be careful in involving with such control freaks. Why? Because friendship becomes dangerous when dominated or controlled by one person. It ceases being a mutual involvement. True friendship involves cooperation rather than coercion, control or domination of others. It is an environment that should provide for growth and development of the involved individuals. They are to grow in trust, loyalty, faithfulness, unselfishness, and adjustment to others' persona and so forth.

From those teachings, Dinah gleaned that truthfulness and faithfulness were some of the noblest virtues of a commendable person. Hence, pursuing friendships to develop such characteristics was considered a God given opportunity. It was a platform for them to learn and grow to appreciate, tolerate, or reaffirm and forgive others; thereby learning to serve, support or help them. From such wisdom she learned that everyone needs a friend or friends, and for that matter; good friends. Yet people who are only out to abuse or exploit others are no good friends.

Friendship provides us opportunities and people we can be honest with, we can freely talk to and eventually build ourselves around. They become a people we can always turn to in times of need; those who can help us, inspire us and even encourage us. A people who will always be there for us. And the freer we get in the friendships the closer we get to each other, and the stronger the relational bonds become. The very spirit of friendship should be the extending of ourselves out to others, thereby releasing us from selfishness that is a trait we all exhibit in different degrees.

These were good virtues; however, these Canaanite girls somewhat had a fixation with boyfriends and sexual love only. They seemed to have bought into the myth that women only find their worth in men's acceptance. That is why they schemed to find themselves men or boys to complement them. Their love and acceptance only came from such boys; yet that was pegged on their abilities to give those boys sex. Essentially, this bespoke that those women were merely such men's object of (lustful) pleasures. Yet nothing can be farther from the truth; no woman's worth is derived from men, more so based on their willingness or ability to give sex. A woman's worth is uniquely in who she is as a person.

Sadly, because of the prevalence of such notions in Canaan, their young women seemed to live only for boys or men's admirations. It was what made them feel worthwhile. They would spend a great deal of time in trying to make themselves appealing to men. They somewhat felt incomplete without boyfriends or men friends. Yet, the palpability of a woman should have begun in her home, rather than with some boyfriend or some man out there.

No wonder, most of those Canaanite girls never pursued relationships for growth and developments in any meaningful way. They got into them marred with selfish affections without the necessary characteristics for proper relationships, resulting in misuse and sometimes abuse. It is like they had no alternatives, but to give in to such unfounded myths thereby lending themselves to the deplorable demands of boys or men's passions. Whereas, in doing that they eventually ended up being alienated from true friendships and the love they so yearned for. That then hindered their truly and fully enjoying their lives. It condemned them to live in the shadows of who they truly were.

So far we have used the term sex a lot in our discussions here, and it is prudent that we define it so we are all clear what we mean by it. Thus, in the next chapter we will do just that. And as usual, let's review first before we do that.

Some Questions to Ponder

1. One of the chapters above is titled "Wisdom from Padan-Aram". What specific thing(s) did you pick up or learned from this wisdom? List and discuss some of them.
2. When Dinah came into the new city she experienced a great deal of cultural differences. Have you personally experienced any cultural differences and how did you deal with them?
3. In the new city Dinah seemed to have had some struggles as she began making friends; what were these? Were such struggles unique to Dinah or they are common to teens everywhere?
4. What good is friendship and why do we need friends anyway? Is it true that friendship among girls is different from their friendship with boys? Explain.
5. Signs of a bad friendship are things like: jealousy, destructive competitions, unfaithfulness, breaking agreements, backbiting, rumor mongering, lying to each other and so forth. Can you explain the reason these are bad for any relationship?
6. Some friends are not good; they hurt others. What are some bad things that friends can do to each

other? Refer to the above question and give personal example if any.
7. Is it easy or difficult to make friends in a new city or environment? Discuss and give reasons.
8. Is it difficult to have true friends, if so explain why? Can you list down people you consider your true friends?

General Meaning of Sex

Dinah was not ignorant as far as facts about sex were concerned. She had grown up in an environment where such matters were no secrets discussed in hushed tones, but were openly conversed about. In fact, sex was considered a "mitzvah"; a good phenomenon originated by Yahweh. This made it easy to discuss more so because they lived in an agrarian and pastoralist society where thousands of animals gave birth day and night. In fact, one of those times when their sheep gave birth; Dinah asked her mother how the sheep got the lamb into her womb. Her mother gave her the necessary information on sexology for her age then, and she kept learning more and more mostly from the grand moms who were charged with such responsibilities.

It was in such a forum that she learned that animals' sexuality is somewhat different from the humans' in that animals only get moved to sex when the female needs to get babies. Whereas human beings get babies via sex, but that is not its sole role in human relationships. Sex in humans is for enjoyment too.

With that explanation we can then begin our definitions of sex. It is what a person is as an outward mark of their being, portraying gender distinctions either as male or female deriving from their specific sexual organs. This simply means that nature through the genitals marks everyone out. In the general traditional understanding, each person is either a male having a penis or a female having a vagina.

Therefore, in simplicity sex is first of all a mark of distinction between the genders (male and female) in creations. Thus, we don't need to be ashamed of being either male or female. Nor should we be ashamed of any of those genitals. They were created and declared good, wonderfully and fearfully made by God Himself. Sadly, today some people tend to shy off or feel embarrassed when sex is mentioned even within a good context. Yet, sex is such a fundamental part of our beings that it does not make any sense to think of it as something bad, or a dirty subject. There is nothing dirty, or bad about sex except when people misuse it and hurt others in the process.

We all are a certain sex, and with proper understanding we can all appreciate that it makes and marks us out for who we are. Particular the genitals are special, specific and important part of the matrix of our human sexuality. Even their locations in the body; their strategic and privileged settings, reveal their preciousness. They are mostly referred to as private parts; seemingly, for the positions they occupy in the body. Apparently, they were designed to be private and hidden except when in use or whenever appropriate.

Like your most valued treasures, they are hidden to portray their preciousness, even though according to Science that is also due to body temperatures and biological functions. Someone observed that such things by their very nature cannot be made common without destroying their values. And by such things he is referring to sex. If we make it common and easy to indulge in, then we lower its preciousness and destroy its worth.

Second, the word sex traditionally means an act that involves a man and a woman expressing their sexuality in using their genitals. This simply means the word sex is both a noun and a verb. As a noun we have seen it is the mark of distinction between male and female, and now as a verb it is the act of expressing sexuality using the genitals. But it is much more than just the bodily functions, because it also carries with it the emotional and spiritual aspects of being.

In its traditional setting it is generally referred to as vaginal intercourse. This is the bringing of the organs together into a union of their functions, with the male organs penetrating into the females'. It is an engagement that functions best only within the bounds of an appropriate mutual relationship called marriage. Yet, this does not mean it cannot be engaged in outside marriage; it can. Yet the fact that it *can be done* outside marriage does not mean *it should be done*. Sex is wrong outside marriage due to several reasons, some stated below.

Arbitrary Sexual Engagements Problematic

Friendship is the platform where many people begin their sexual experiences. As a platform, friendship is a basis for relationships but sex was not designed for it. Sex is wrong in friendships outside of marriage. This is because friendship is just the beginning of an incomplete relationship, which in many cases may never fully develop and can end any time. And when it ends after you have sexually involved with someone, it opens you up to living with long term regrets and coping with difficult emotions.

Some young people argue that since they will marry someday, what harm is there if they have sex in their supposed love? But there are lots of harm; theirs is still an unconfirmed and incomplete relationship. They are still trying to discover each other, and sex in such an environment will always breed psychological problems involving fears and restlessness that tend towards guilt and negative emotions.

Accordingly, sex is not only fun and enjoyable; it is also problematic if not handle appropriately with the care it deserves. Folks who focus only on deriving enjoyment from it often get disillusioned, as it mostly turns into a self-gratifying feat rather than the whole-personality involvement it should be. They are then dogged with the yearnings to change partners, peradventure they may attain that feeling still missing from their involvements with those others. Yet, theirs is a sexual performance divorced from their personalities; just a game they play with whomsoever and whenever they so want. Eventually, it breeds confusions and heartaches rather than the enjoyment it is supposed to bring.

Indeed, as has been repeated, sex is more than just a physical act. It involves the joining of hearts and minds in emotional exchange of energies as couples get lost into each other. That they do in thought, attitude and feelings, and they become deeply intertwined such that they begin feeling indebted to each other. In fact, they begin to feel as if they own each other.

This in them then results in desires and demands for accountability and transparency, more so in relational matters. They begin to want to know what you were doing with so and so, and so forth. As those you have sexually involved with they begin to feel like they have a right to every inch of your life. That simply means, sex is also a means to deep bond and non-verbal communications that should result into genuine intimacy and appreciations of each other. That is why it is usually emotionally devastating to be torn apart from those you have involved with sexually. As has been said, sex forms a bond; yet, a bond without commitment is a recipe for untold heartaches.

In its design, sex is for the enjoyment of those who have chosen to lock themselves into each other's life through the bond of their unswerving commitments. Indeed, that is what marriage is; the committing of one's life and happiness to the retention of another. It is a platform where they are to work out their relationship in pleasuring each other, as they grow in oneness as a fully committed couple. It is the yielding of one fully to each other; the surrender of their body, soul and every emotion to their spouse; the blissful losing of themselves into their partner just like the day light disappears into the night.

And the creator intended it to be so as a means of bringing the couples into an intimacy of being deep in the other, and shallow in themselves. This can only be experienced in unswerving commitment and a responsive reciprocation of passion, and complementarity that then becomes the profound celebration of their lives forever.

That is why the highly promoted self-sex (masturbation or toy sex) of today is nothing but guilt-prone lonely, shallow and an unfulfilling hollow experiences. There is no responsive reciprocation of passion; there is no love partnership nor kindred souls to double and share in the joy of sex. It is a fleeting exercise, a sex without friendship or any fondness with a shared tender feelings.

Mostly, individuals peevishly and selfishly try to pleasure their renegade human natures and perverse desires, but without adding to the felicity of a fellow human being. Instead of fulfilling and bringing them the joys they so desire; it instead alienates them leaving them with horrible, gloomy and guilty feelings. Of course, it is riddled with hollowness and embarrassment as there is no embrace or commitment of another.

It is thus, important to reiterate that sex is not just a game for young people to play; it can make or wreck one's life indefinitely. It is a force of its own that only functions best within the bounds of a lifelong right relationship called marriage. Without the life-long commitment that binds you together, sexual involvement ceases from being a celebration and an enjoyment, to being an emotional experimentation by two persons trying to belong to each other. And in most cases, such experimentations usually turn sour and eventually poison the very relationships they are supposed to galvanize. It leads to jealousy, rivalry and violent lustful passions; not forgetting deceit, worries and restlessness and other unnecessary anxieties involving excessive emotional self-consciousness.

There are always uncomfortable and uneasy feelings associated with sex in every non-guaranteed and insecure relationships. This is because it involves the exchanges of life energies that destroy its very beauty and joy when it is treated improperly. It turns into unfulfilling and a meaningless adventure of trying to derive pleasure from it without real regards to its true nature and worth.

No wonder the Good Book says, "It is God's will that you should be sanctified: that you should avoid sexual immorality; that each of you should learn to control his (or her) own body in a way that is holy and honorable, not in passionate lust like heathens, who do not know God; and in this matter no one should wrong his (or her) brother or take advantage of him (or her). . . For God did not call us to be impure, but to live a holy life." And in some other place it says, "Let us behave decently, as in the daytime, not in orgies and drunkenness, not in sexual immorality and debauchery, not in dissension and jealousy."

Naturally, sexual intercourse plants male seeds inside a female partner. Every time there is a natural sexual union taken to its conclusion, male seeds are in most cases released into the involved female. (Though in the modern times there are thin plastic or rubber bags called condoms that are used to trap such seed, but the fact remains that male seed leave the male body). These seeds are called sperms, which are made from the male's blood system and carry with them some inherent diseases in the man if any. This is the reason sexual involvements are the major sources of some Sexually Transmitted Infectious (STI) diseases like the Chlamydia, Syphilis and Gonorrhea, Herpes and many others including the incurable AIDS.

However, even just by the fact that there is usually some kind of bodily fluid exchanges in the traditional sexual intercourse, shouldn't girls be wise enough to be bothered by who should contribute such releases into them? Why should they allow every Tom, Dick and Harry to release such fluids into them? Why let everyone have the very best of their valuables? Aware of it or not, women who sleep around with everyone are cheapening themselves; they lower their dignity! They may have their reasons, but those don't change the facts. Sleeping with men arbitrarily takes away from their dignity anyhow.

No wonder, the young Jewish women in Padan-Aram were taught to know better and carry themselves with the highest dignity they deserved. They were not to buy into the myth that giving sex makes a woman attractive. A woman is already attractive because of who she is, not because she can give sex. To give sex so as to be attractive was unfounded claim.

As unique young women those girls owed no man sex, and their attractiveness derived from many other sources other than just sex. Even today, girls are to be wisely aware that they owe no man sex. They ought to stand up and be counted as good stewards of the wonderful gift of their bodies granted them by the creator. Every girl needs to understand they are uniquely special and should not mindlessly submit to lustful men, only interested in their bodies and just want to use them. Of course, no man is entitled to any woman's body except his wife's, and only with the wife's consent and considerations.

Clearly, every (young) woman is special and that is one of the reasons men or young men will always admire them. They are *woo – men*; made to woo the men. But their specialness is not just about their physical attractions only. That is where the weight has been put over the years. Yet there is more to a woman than just her looks. Women are the aggregate of who they really are; including their invisible emotional and intellectual connections that are unconsciously part of their beings. There is tremendous worth in every woman's life just by the virtue of who they are.

Thus, women need this understanding so that they can carry themselves with much dignity and purity that their worthwhile lives deserve. No woman is just a sexual object; they are persons of value and grace. Thus, no woman should be at any man's or anyone's beck and call. They should do themselves a favor by refusing to be manipulated, exploited or misused by anyone. Moreover, they should work to preserve their self-respects and uphold their dignities by recognizing and respecting who they really are. Subsequently, they must not dish out their erogenous treasures to everyone that comes along. That is how they will safeguard their uniqueness and preserve their valuable personal histories.

Dinah and her peers in Padan-Aram learned that young people, especially women deserve better. They need to be valued, respected and appreciated. Yet that respect begins with them. They must respect themselves first, then others will respect them too. They share in the highest privilege of being humans with eternal values enshrined in their live to elevate and dignify them. They, therefore, need to keep Yahweh's high standards and live positively.

The Good Book puts it that God wants them to be holy, and not to be immoral in matters of sex. They should respect and honor their bodies, by not letting themselves become slaves to their natural desires, which can make them live like people who don't know or don't care about God.

Some Questions to Ponder

1. Is it important to learn about sex or have sex education at all, or is sex a private matter that should be left to individuals to discover for themselves? Explain your answer
2. Where and who should be involved in sex education if at all it should be undertaken, and what should be some of the topics taught? Discuss.
3. Does learning about sex reduce or increase the chances of sexual experimentations among the young people? Discuss
4. Why are there little discussions on sex related matters between children and their parents? How can this be overcome?
5. Why are young people cautioned against sexual involvements before the appropriate times?
6. What would you say about physical contacts in the form of kissing and the like in young people's involvements; should it be encouraged or not and if so, how far?
7. Should young people be exposed to explicit sexual situations; say RR-rated movies and video games,

inappropriate TV programs, pornography and so forth as means of encouraging them to learn sexual matters? Give reasons for your answer.
8. How about the theory that there is much information out there and young people will just learn in one way or the other; is this a healthy approach? Explain.
9. Sex is not just a physical act. Do you agree or disagree? Explain

Dinah and Shechem's Conversations

As they left Tina's residence, Shechem engaged Dinah in a number of questions so as to set their conversations rolling.

"So how do you find life here in Canaan; do you like it here better than Haran, Ms Dinah?"

"To me life here is just like in any other place and of course, I do like it here." Answered Dinah.

"How about your family, especially your brothers; do they like it here too?" Shechem further enquired.

"Yeah, I believe they do except during our first days when they had not adjusted to life here" Dinah explained.

"So what do you do here at Tina's; I gather you come often?" Shechem asked.

"As you know, Tina is my friend and so even if we don't have anything to do I can always visit her. But to answer your question, we really have nothing specific that we do. We just hang out together and sometimes I help her with chores as we chat." Dinah responded.

"Oh, that's good of you. Now, let's talk about you."

"What about me!" Dinah interrupted.

"I simply want to know you. And there is no better way of doing so than you telling me." Shechem responded.

"So what do you want to know about me?" Dinah posed.

"Everything, but let's start with your looks. I guess you resemble someone in your family, but I cannot say who. Do you resemble anyone at all, or my guess is totally off?" Shechem asked.

"When people see us they say I resemble my mother, but I do not think so." Dinah responded, and then asked, "How come you ask, do I seem to look like someone you know, or have seen somewhere?"

"Not really, it just occurred to me that your beautiful face must be after some relative of yours." Shechem responded.

Then his questions continued becoming more personal, especially about who she was; where they came from, how life was there and so forth. On her part she felt it was difficult to talk about herself and so she just told him about her brothers.

"Are your brothers protective?" Shechem finally asked her.

"Like in what? What do you mean?" She asked.

"Protective ... that is always watching over you."

"I don't know," she answered.

"How are they? Or rather what kind of brothers are they?" Shechem enquired further.

"They are very much like any brothers. They are nice just like brothers should be and I believe they too will be glad to meet you." Dinah intimated.

Eventually their conversations got down to love and personal feelings, something like:

"Has anyone told you how lovely you are?" Shechem asked

"Yes, my brothers tell me that all the times." Dinah responded.

"Whoa, your brothers seem to be a wonderful lot then," said Shechem.

"Yes, they are. Why do you ask?" enquired Dinah.

"First, let me rephrase my question." Shechem chipped in. "Has anyone told you they love you?"

"Of course yes, I have told you my brothers tell me that all the times. "Why do you ask?" Dinah insisted.

"Not for anything," answered Shechem. "I am just curious because of your charming beauty. By the way, do you realize how cute you are! I think every young man would be interested in you."

"Thanks for your compliments." Dinah responded as she added, "You know I am still new here and the more friends I have, the better; I will learn my way around much quicker."

"I hope you would not mind if I personally tell you that I love you, and that I want you to be my girl. I trust that is all right with you."

"Who said it is all right with me? Don't put words in my mouth." Dinah responded straightaway.

"Does that offend you?" Shechem queried her.

"Why should I be offended when someone says they love me, unless you mean something else?" Countered Dinah.

"No. I do not have any other meaning, but that I love you." Shechem reiterated.

"Thank you for your love, but I find it strange here in Canaan that you people talk a lot about love, love; with everyone saying I love you, I love you. What does that even mean? Can't you people find something else to talk about?" Dinah asked sarcastically.

"What else is there to talk about in this world if you cannot talk about love, especially love for someone as dear as you?" Shechem responded to her question.

"I get flattered when people begin talking like this," responded Dinah.

"What do you mean, don't you know that love is the coolest thing in the whole world, a feeling you need in your life and especially given by someone like me who really loves you?" Shechem answered.

"Is that a joke or are you kidding me?" Retorted Dinah angrily.

"Oh Di; excuse me, can I call you Di?" Requested Shechem.

"What is wrong with my full name Dinah? Why, do you want to shorten it; don't you like it as it is?" Dinah asked.

"Not really, but it sounds more special to me when I shorten it into Di," Shechem answered.

"All right then, please yourself. It is fine with me, but I do not like your innuendoes about loving me" Dinah responded.

"There is nothing wrong in my loving you; someone has got to love somebody anyway. That is the reason the earth goes round. And as a girl you need to be loved tenderly and wonderfully, and I am the one who can do that adequately." Explained Shechem.

"My brothers love me all the times, why in particular do you think you are the one qualified to love me any better?" Dinah posed.

"Because I love you." Shechem replied.

"What do you mean you love me?" Dinah asked.

"What do I mean? Don't you know what it means to be loved, or are you already offended because I told you so?" Shechem asked, somewhat trying to bring himself to understand her.

"Not at all, why should I be offended?" Dinah responded. "I just do not seem to get what you mean because everybody here seems to be fascinated with saying I love you. It is just a cliché."

"All right then, what I am saying is that I feel we have such a good connection; there is a wonderful chemistry working between us that we should do something about." Shechem explained.

"What do you mean good chemistry and all that stuff about you and me? What are you getting at?" Dinah asked.

"That simply means we should respond to our feelings for each other." Shechem told her.

"I don't have any feelings for you, so speak for yourself." Dinah pointed out.

"It is not up to me to convince you of the feelings I know you have for me Di. But I should make you aware that your beauty and charm caught my attention the very first day I saw you. That's the reason I am here." Shechem stated as he moved closer to her.

Dinah thought he was flattering her and did not know what to make of that statement. She somewhat stared blankly into space still thinking of how to respond when Shechem continued.

"You know when I first saw you, my heart skipped and I realized how special you are, especially to me; your beauty overwhelmed me and caught me in the grip of admiration."

"Are you being poetic now?" Dinah asked.

"No, I am just telling you the truth. In fact, I am still in the grip of your beauty. I fell in love with you the moment I saw you. I had to find you and let you know how my heart feels about you. You are a wonderful person. This is why I wish to be with you; I want you in my life." Shechem continued.

"Do not flatter me please." Dinah said contemptuously.

"Of course, you are most beautiful Di; very special and beautiful. I like you, especially your eyes and your smile; seeing you makes me feel wonderful. I know you can thrill my heart, and as such I need you to be my girl like I have told you. That is what I mean." Shechem elaborated.

"Yes, I know I am beautiful, but what does that have to do with any of our conversations here?" Dinah responded.

Shechem disregarded her question. He stopped her and looked her in the eyes and said, "I truly love you Di, and I have begun imagining several wonderful possibilities for us. In fact, I have good feelings for our future."

"Keep your imaginations to yourself, I am not interested in any of it." Dinah told him off.

As they came behind the scrubs on the wayside, Shechem quickly placed his arms on her shoulders and pulled her close to him. Before she knew it he moved his hands tenderly to her waist, and then grabbed her and kissed her lips while stroking her hair.

"Yuck, what are you doing? Is something wrong with you? Do not touch me like that. Please, stop your uncouth actions toward me," demanded Dinah pushing him a way. "If you do that again, I will walk away. Let's just talk; no touching, no kissing or anything. I hardly know you," she continued sternly in the wake of his advances.

Yet he downplayed her warnings and instead complimented her saying, "Wow, I even like your hair too, you have got such nice hair that makes you look really special. Indeed, you are truly amazing and should appreciate that you are this beautiful."

But Dinah also ignored his compliments. She was angry at the way he had behaved toward her, kissing and touching her anyhow. She had been taught that love between two people was not just a matter of kissing or caressing, but should be true expression of concern and goodwill toward each other. It is not a one sided affairs. It was rightfully so that she recognized Shechem's touch as inappropriate at that point.

Unfortunately, some young people do not seem to understand the power of touch or the fact that there is good and bad touch. Physical touch can spark an emotional flame of affection at an inappropriate time in young people's lives that may eventually derail their ability to stay morally pure and strong. There is a touch that arouses strong sexual emotions and once aroused they abhor control. They would want to be channeled to their specific logical ends, which may not be appropriate in friendships.

Wisdom has it that no one can put a burning coal or charcoal on their chests and expect not to be burned! It has been pointed out that much of youthful touch is usually without commitment of true love. It often ends with the young woman held in the embrace of the philandering.

Therefore, it is important to encourage young people to be conservative in regards to physical touch and affections, before they set on the path to serious relationships towards marriage. However, that is not to condemn physical touch wholesale; it is only to inform the young people of the power inherent in physical affections. It is strong and it might easily and unintendedly sweep them off their moral standing. Yet, any defeat in this area will linger on with them for years to come. In some cases, the defeat may hinder their ability to live freely and happily later in marriage.

Like was in Shechem's case, sometimes it begins with innocently placing one's arms on the shoulders of another. But those hands may soon find their way down to the breasts and before the young people know it, the hands may move to the private parts. Yet in such cases young people should still be in a position to say no and mean it, especially the girls.

Hence, as much as possible young people need to cultivate self-control and sensibility in taking a stand for decency and moral uprightness. Particularly when they are alone, young people should be the most cautious. They must make the necessary sacrifices now, secured in piety. That is what Dinah did here, but Shechem with his own selfish intentions countered her as they were coming out from behind the shrubbery.

"Di, I just want to assure you of my love; in fact, I love you more than you really know." Shechem said.

"When did you start loving me; you do not even know me how can you claim to love me?" Dinah countered.

"But Di you have just told me all about yourself; do you still think I do not know you!" Shechem wondered.

"I think we should change our conversations to another topic." Responded Dinah.

"Is there anything wrong in our talking about love, and in this case my love for you?" Shechem asked.

"No, there is nothing wrong in talking about love, but in our case I just don't see where this is going right now. It feels to me like we are wasting time talking of irrelevant things." Dinah told him.

"What is irrelevant about our talks?"

"It seems to me you can take advantage of others by your type of talks. But it is wrong to do so." Dinah expressed.

"Oh sweet Di, you know I cannot do such a thing. Why should I take advantage of anyone?" Shechem responded.

"The way you are talking does not feel right to me. Love is not something to be entered into this lightly." Dinah clarified.

"Yes, I know love is a serious involvement and I am glad you too know this. Moreover, I see you reason so maturely; I cannot imagine my life without you, where have you been all this time?" Shechem asked.

"Your life without me, what do you mean? Supposing you never met me at all what would you have done?" enquired Dinah.

"All that is just a supposition Di, you are now here and you know I love you." Shechem responded trying to convince her of his love.

"I think I do not want to talk about this anymore; can we talk about something else?" Dinah expressed.

"Does that mean you do not need my love?" Shechem asked pretending to be surprised.

"Not really, but who said I needed it in the first place?" Responded Dinah. "You pretend to know love, but talk like you don't know anything about it and that makes me uneasy. Love takes time to be properly developed and responded to." Dinah pointed out.

Then she continued, "It is only through such a process that people can really get to know each other. Right now I do not know you and you do not know me. I, therefore, think it is a mistake for us to be talking about love. Please, let us talk about something else." She begged.

But Shechem could neither change his mind nor the subject. He liked the way things seemed to be going so far. By then they had reached the eastern end of Canaan Gateway Park. Leaving the Park behind, they crossed over to the Mayor's Street as they continued with their conversations. Shechem then decided to go show her his home just a few meters or so down the end of that lane.

"That is true Di; but like I told you earlier, I feel like I have known you all my life. I now just need to express my love to you in a practical way." Shechem told her.

"And how do you intend to do that? Are you not expressing love even as we talk and walk together, or what love are you talking about?" Dinah asked kind of astonished.

"Why are you just countering everything I say Di; why do you want to sound ridiculous? Don't you know that a love like ours can only be expressed fully when we make love?" Shechem tried making his intentions plain.

"You sound more ridiculous than I; what are you getting at by your statement express love making love?" Dinah countered.

"That simply means we have got to have sex; I need to discover you so I can feel the warmth between your. . . you know, and then just lie there feeling your body close to mine." Shechem explained.

"Aauwi! Be ashamed of yourself. Can't you give me some respect! What are you talking about, don't be obnoxious; are you crazy? How can you say such things to me? Who do you think I am?" Dinah exclaimed.

"Not so fast my dear; why are you so alarmed?" enquired Shechem.

"I tell you I am not going to take any more of this nonsense. Take me back to Tina's." Dinah demanded.

"Why my dear; did I say anything strange?" Shechem asked.

"No, not strange but unkind and inappropriate at this point. Furthermore, I think this is not the time to talk about such things. What do you know about sex?" she asked derisively.

"Don't be ridiculous Di; what do you mean by your question? A girl like you, with your kind of looks should not ask such a question! Don't you know that sex is fun and the most enjoyable involvement in life that every person deserves? Everything in life is about it; even the way you dress and so forth. You do not need to know anything about it; you only need to enjoy it. It is not a lesson to be learnt, but an experience to be enjoyed." Shechem lectured her.

"Oh no, I cannot buy into that. You are wrong and disrespectful of me for that matter," she interjected. "Does that mean love is synonymous with sex to you? You have been talking much about love when in essence you meant sex; how ridiculous! Does it then mean when you look at me, you only see me in terms of sex? Is that how you see women, and is it right for you to only look at women in terms of sex?" Continued Dinah angrily.

"That is not the case my dear, why are you talking of women when this conversation is just between you and me? Remember I have told you how beautiful you are to me and you need to be loved carefully, purposefully and intimately. And that is what I desire to do." Shechem responded.

"I am not interested in that kind of love," retorted Dinah. "You have not even answered my question if love to you is synonymous with sex?" She added.

"Let's not waste time arguing over the semantics. One thing you should know is that I love you." Shechem said trying to calm her down.

"But I have told you I am not interested in that kind of love; a love that does not respect me, does not appeal to reasons and uses foul language. Such a love makes fatuous relationships." She explained.

Shechem bombarded by Dinah's astonishing stand voiced his concern. "Di, you should know we do not have time for all these kinds of arguments now. The time we have in our hands is for loving each other. I hate it when love-birds like us waste time arguing when we can readily experience our love."

"If you are only after experience then yours is only an infatuation and I am not ready for any of that." Dinah pointed out.

Dinah neither appreciated nor accepted Shechem's approach in trying to woo her to be his love. He claimed to love her so much, yet to her it was provocative and disrespectful talk on their first encounter. They had just met and hardly knew each other. To her, premature talks about love and sex were just infatuations that could lead to irresponsible lifestyles. And if it were today, Shechem's verbal innuendos would have squarely qualified for sexual harassments.

Thus, unlike some young people who grow up without proper information on sex and love; Dinah seemed to have learnt a lot. Therefore, she refused to be zapped into Shechem's appeal to her beauty through the unconfirmed expression of verbal love. Indeed, Shechem used the expression "I love you" a lot in trying to convince her, but she refused. However, sometimes knowledge alone is not enough, but how it is used or employed.

It has been observed that sometimes a man will say he cares about a girl or that he loves her, but he'll admit he's not "in love" with her. Because there is a difference between someone loving you and being in love with you. Unfortunately, many a times our young people do not seem to know the difference.

Generally, love is more than what a person says; more than their smiles. Love is who they really are in the inside that can be manifested in their actions of kindness and respect toward you.

Some Questions to Ponder

1. Based on the information you have gathered so far, what sort of a person do you think Shechem was? What seemed to have been his main focus in life? Discuss
2. There is always the tendency of touching and holding each other in young people's relationships. Discuss touching in relation to youth sexuality. Is there good and bad touch? How can one differentiate?
3. The word love is commonly and freely thrown about nowadays to express personal feelings towards others, and it seems it has been abused or

misused. What is your understanding of the word love? When someone tells you they love you, what exactly do you understand they mean? Discuss

4. The author states that there is a difference between someone loving you and being in love with you. Do you agree? Explain the differences.
5. Dinah desired to change the topic of their conversations. How would changing the subject have helped? Why do you think Shechem refused to change their conversation? Discuss.
6. In the course of their exchanges with Shechem about love, Dinah seemingly understood that he was equating love with sex. Was her understanding right? Explain
7. Dinah asked Shechem, if indeed he was only seeing her in terms of sex. What do you think she meant? Are there people who look at others in terms of sex rather than in terms of their persons? Explain
8. Unfortunately, some men look at women only in terms of their bodily features like their breasts; should this even be the case? What does this tell us about such people?

In Shechem's Home

Finally, they reached Shechem's residence, which comprised of, among others, a greyish mud-brick house that was gorgeous inside but did not attract much attention from the outside. Shechem took her straight to his room where they were to continue their conversations.

Although Dinah had refused Shechem's flirtatious advances and an appeal about his love for her; somehow, she naively accepted to go to his home and into his room. By the way his room was slightly detached from the main brick building housing his parents. When they got into his room Dinah felt like something was amiss and she began freaking out in the inside, although she put on a brave face. She straightway proceeded to the window across the other end of the room, trying to steady herself.

In the meantime, Shechem closed and locked the door behind them as she was engrossed in scanning the room. In fact, she hardly noticed him lock the door. From her scanning of the room, it was a pleasant spacious and medially furnished room. It looked comfortable, having a gorgeous animal skin rag covering the floor. It was hung with some old tapestry and an old portrait lined one of the walls, with a pendant on the other. But then Shechem interrupted her thoughts by saying,

"All right Di, here we are; welcome to my room. Feel free and be yourself."

"Your room is fabulous," Dinah said

"Was it a gift for winning something or just the generosity of your dad? I bet your dad must be a well-to-do citizen," Dinah said pretending not to know anything about his father.

Just then without answering her specific question Shechem said, "Let's get back to the last point of our discussions on our way here. What did you tell me about love?"

"I thought we finished with that topic." Dinah responded. "Can we talk about something else; in fact, can you tell me more about yourself and your room?" She added continuing to stare out of the window.

"Let's finish with first things first," commanded Shechem speaking with an authoritative voice as he moved toward her.

Sensing Shechem moving towards her, she broke into cold sweat feeling the hair on the back of her head rising. But he simply leaned forward and looked her in the eyes insisting they should finish with their talks on love. He seemed very determined about it and he asked her,

"What's your last word on love?"

Dinah recollected herself and boldly repeated her earlier statement saying, "I maintain I am not interested in unreasonable love".

But Shechem kind of offended that a girl could talk to him like that asked her, "Why are you talking to me like that my dear; is my love for you unreasonable? Is that how you feel?"

He seemed a little intimidated by her straight talks as if she was his equal. He had always carried himself as superior to everyone in that city, and so he was surprised that this new girl did not take cognizance of that fact. He seemed to mistakenly believe that boys (more so his class) were superior to girls and hence, a girl should not have spoken to him a certain way. To him girls did not have the right to free expression in front of young men like him. Yet that is a patriarchal demeaning outlook that must never be entertained whatsoever.

Nevertheless, in terms of general relationships all young people feel the same emotions, ranging from yearning for acceptance to fears and insecurities both imagined and true. Boys are no better than girls in this regard. Thus, it is unfortunate to suppose that they are superior to girls. No wonder, nursing such unfounded superiority feelings; Shechem was bothered by Dinah's forthrightness. He then moved closer to and held her once again looking her in the eyes saying;

"I am sorry Di, I did not mean to hurt your feelings or anything."

"No, no; do not touch me like that. I thought we agreed you will not touch me again!" Dinah objected angrily pushing him away.

"I am doing this just to reassure you of my love. Looking at you sends sensational pulses throughout my body and makes me want you the more; you know. I hope I have not hurt your feelings." Shechem said.

"It is not about my feelings, but about your attitude." Dinah said kind of telling him off.

"What about my attitude?" enquired Shechem.

"It is horrible, I do not like it; it is starting to make me feel sick." answered Dinah shaking her head.

"I am sorry my dear; I did not bring you here to make you sick, but to love you." expressed Shechem.

And he then grabbed her suddenly, pulling her toward him and kissing her again. She felt like she would faint. Her knees felt weak, but somehow she struggled and broke loose from him. Frightened, she ran to the door only to find it locked.

"Oh, my goodness," She exclaimed in dismay, shocked to learn that he had even locked the door.

"Can you please open this door or I will scream?" She threatened while pounding on the door. "Why did you lock it in the first place?" She asked angrily.

Instantly, many thoughts began crossing her mind and her heart began to race. She imagined that Shechem might have had some ulterior motives, since he even locked the door. She thought about her family; her dad and brothers. She was terrified and worried. What would she do? She wondered inwardly. Her instinct told her that something terrible might happen to her, and at such a thought she exclaimed;

"Please do not hurt me." She said this with a strange edge to her voice.

"Take it easy Di; you know I would never hurt you." Shechem said trying to calm her down. He then walked toward the door pretending he was going to unlock it. But then to her dismay he surprisingly grabbed her again. She protested even hitting him with her fists trying to break free, but to no avail. He held her tightly and lifted her off her feet.

Dinah was about five feet or something; weighing about a hundred or slightly fewer pounds. Whereas, Shechem was a tall (about six something), muscled individual more heavily built weighing somewhere between one hundred eighty to two hundred (180-200) pounds. He felt that since Dinah had accepted to come to his home and into his room, she must have consented to his unwelcome, unexpressed and unexplained desires.

In other words, he presumed she was equally interested in having sex with him. This led to his misguided conclusion that he was then entitled to proceed to sexual intercourse with her even if through humiliation. He intended to finish his conquest of her by asserting his masculinity through that sexual intercourse. He felt he was entitled to it as the man or *the head* of that relationship. Of course, he was in charge of that whole situation, and he quickly moved from seduction to coercion and intimidation. However, he was awfully wrong; he misread Dinah's intentions.

Some Questions to Ponder

1. Is it wise to intentionally isolate yourself with a person of the opposite sex, especially those you

may have feelings for, even if you think you cannot go overboard? Explain
2. When Shechem said, "Let's finish with first things first." What do you think he meant? And in whose agenda was it first?
3. Why is it necessary to clearly communicate your feelings and desires in a mutual relationship?
4. What is your take on this line from one of the paragraphs above: In terms of relationships, all young people feel the same emotions ranging from yearning for acceptance to fears and insecurities both imagined and true. Boys are no better than girls in this regard. Are boys superior to girls in any way? Discuss giving relevant examples if any.
5. If you feel you are at cross-purposes with your friend like it seemed Dinah felt when she wanted to change the topic of their conversation; what is the best cause of action?
6. When we wrong our friends and we realize it, what should we do? Why is that important?

Dinah Unexpectedly Defiled

Dinah neither solicited nor consented to Shechem's behavior towards her, even though he presumed it was his way of showing her or expressing his love. Dinah did not sanction it, and he could not understand why she was trying to play a saint by being all worked up and upset over his advances. To him, she willfully came to his home and into his room and that was a sign enough she was ready for him. But was that really the case? Of course not.

Dinah was bewildered; she did not imagine Shechem could even think of doing such a thing to her. They hardly knew each other and even if they did it was not the right time. It did not occur to her that sex would be the next immediate thing to face in her involvement with Shechem. In fact, they had not even talked or worked out any conditions under which sex, if at all, could take place. She was caught unawares in the morass of things. There were many things she would have liked to talk to him about, but then she felt intimidated and inadequate to do so. She had a sinking feeling in the pit of her stomach.

She had hoped like Tina had informed her that Shechem was a gentleman and that he would act gently. However, from his inconsistent actions toward her that far; she concluded he was not. Or was he only playing? However, she refused to play along with his demands and to her dismay Shechem grabbed her and lifted her off her feet as we have observed above.

"Please, stop. Put me down. What are you doing?" Dinah demanded swinging her feet.

Shechem totally ignored her and she could not believe it; it was like a bad dream. Anyway, when he put her down; it was on the bed, and he pushed her on it and pinned her down there.

"Can I ask you something please?" She said twisting and turning. But Shechem had a strong grip on her.

"Please, stop. Are you serious, what are you doing?" Dinah cried out pleading with him.

Shechem continued ignoring her. He was dead serious; sex with her was his ultimate goal. He presumed that if he started it, Dinah would play along. His idea was that having sex was then the next normal and desirable thing for them as a people who appeared to love each other. But he was reasoning from his own perspective. His determination to have sex with her, in the name of making love, did not care the least about her own desires and personal feelings about it.

He was so used to getting his way in life that he did not consider it wrong to violate Dinah, or any woman for that matter. Therefore, he went ahead and undid his pants; then he pushed Dinah's skirt up and forcefully parted her legs, after which he tore her underpants and penetrated into her.

"Oh, my God!" She exclaimed holding her breath as she felt him in her. She tried pushing and fighting him off, hitting him with her fists. But all that did not deter him.

"No-o-o-o-o, my goodness. I can't believe this. Please stop! You are hurting me. Get off me. Please stop, please don't do this to me." She pleaded.

"How can you do such a thing to me? You said you loved me; is this the love you were talking about? Why don't we talk first?" Cried Dinah with a numbness of feelings, trying to push him off. She then ordered him saying, "Get off me; you're hurting me. Please, leave me alone. Don't touch me anymore."

But Shechem, a lusty demeaning, hedonistic and unapologetic aggressive young man did not care the least about her; he just continued his unwarranted and unwelcome business. Whereas, Dinah with a flood of tears streaming down her cheeks tried screaming, but seemingly no sound came out. Yet somehow some sound did. But in the meantime she began regretting, even wishing she hadn't accepted his invitation in the first place.

Yet, Shechem engrossed in his beastly selfish escapade continued to abuse her without any remorse. He took what he wanted from her with no regards to her wellbeing or feelings. It was all just about him: his desires, pleasures and fun. Dinah was just an object he used towards that end. He seemed to like sex just for its own sake and neither for the woman nor relationship's sake. He supposed that Dinah "had made her bed and so had to lie in it" – even though from the look of things, she did not want to be laid on any bed!

Oh, what a situation! It was appallingly horrible; she was being raped openly and there was nothing she could do about it. What a helpless situation; she felt hopeless and awfully out of control. Thoughts began running wild in her mind. She felt like her life was over. That was it. What would she do? Or where would she go? Crawl away and hide forever, or run off to some unknown destinations never to be seen or heard from again.

Whoa, how dirty and useless she felt. The sense of defilement and impurity came upon her like an enveloping veil. How could this happen to her when she had always been a nice caring and respectful girl. She did not do the things the Canaanite girls did. In fact, she did not even have a boyfriend! It had never occurred to her, like is common with some people, that rape can happen to anybody.

"Oh, no-o-o-o," she continued sobbing and crying. She indeed cried uncontrollably, even as Shechem tried to quieten her down. When she could not stop crying, he leaped off the bed when he finished his dirty business and stood barefoot next to it. He then commanded her saying, "You can now cover yourself and stop that silly game of crying. You look so ridiculous crying like a child."

He was trying to intimidate and make her feel guilty for crying, but she refused and kept on crying the more. Since she did not obey him to stop crying, he considered that a defiance. He then authoritatively ordered her to leave his room. But she declined that order also.

"I would rather die here than go anywhere; for your information I am going nowhere," retorted Dinah in a defiant faint voice in the midst of her sobs. "I cannot imagine how cruel you are. What have you just done to me and then you are talking to me like that; you do not even seem to see anything wrong?" Dinah added angrily.

"You only have yourself to blame girl, if you feel that what we have done is wrong." Shechem told her with a wry of a smile on his face.

"You did with who? Don't claim that we did anything. You did it all by yourself. Unceremoniously, abusing and hurting me with disregard to my pleas that you stop. I did not do anything with you." Dinah retorted.

"I don't know about that girl." Shechem responded and then added, "What I know is that we have made love and that is what you needed."

Seemingly, Shechem had intended to use his position as the mayor's son to manipulate and intimidate Dinah. He wanted to control the situation as if nothing bad had happened. It was all about frightening Dinah to dance to his tunes. His disrespect for women made him subjugate and sexually abuse this innocent young woman. He did not understand that Dinah was not making it up; it was true he had inhumanly violated her and violently taken away her virginity and dignity. She was emotionally and even physically hurt; she was bleeding profusely and she needed care and attention.

But Shechem had no real regards for her; he thought he had the right to force himself on her, because she had come into his room. However, nobody has that right regardless of where the woman is; no one has the right to exploit others, more so, sexually. No man or boy has the right to force a girl (woman) into sexual intercourse with them. It is not only immoral, but it is criminal too. Such violations and abstracted sexual acts are not what any woman deserves. Every woman, like everyone else, deserves better and proper treatment involving love, respect and honor.

However, Shechem opted for rape; a heinous act that is the use of one's power over another to forcefully involve them into a romantic or sexual involvement without their express consent. It is a rough and offensive hideous mechanical approach to sex, perpetrated by those brute persons who lack the grace or charm to amicably approach or seduce others. They have their own insecurities and go about proving themselves the wrong way. They approach seduction with a battle-mentality presuming they have to physically conquer the victim and break down their resistances. They hurt others to prove or to feel powerful, but it is what reveals their weaknesses.

Rape, therefore, is not so much about sex as it is about violence and cruelty to and the subjugation of others. It is a symbol of abuse and a violation of other people's psyche and bodies. It is an insensitive, retrogressive and uncouth act to be perpetrated on other human beings. It has nothing to do with love; if you love people you don't rape or perpetrate such a violent act on them. In fact, it is solely done for the sexual gratification of the person using force. That is why I say there is no love in rape. No considerations are given to the feelings or desires, or even the physical conditions of the victim(s) being forced into the sexual act.

It did not matter that Dinah had gone with Shechem to his home and then into his room. The sense of respect both self-respect and respect for the girl, and the desire to build a long lasting relationship should have guided him. Where was his self-respect and self-control? It is unfortunate he let himself be led by his un-girdled red hot lustful emotions, which then landed him into that predicament. He wanted to be accepted and he presumed that by doing that to Dinah; she would want him more. But he was wrong, "having sex" does not prove or produce love if love is not there in the first place.

In the wider scheme of things; Shechem gave up his long-term dream of becoming the next mayor or some great person in his society for a short-term thrill. The lure of sex with its strong feelings excited his mind, and by inconsideration and rashness he undertook the act at the wrong time and in unwelcome manner involving humiliation.

It has been stated that if one does not control his or her sexual appetite, it will eventually control him or her. And they cannot imagine what that may result into! In most cases, it leads them into forfeiting the glories of true and blessed relationships for a momentary intercourse that then affects their welfare for many years to come.

With Dinah lying on his bed confused and bleeding, Shechem needed to come up with a solution as quickly as possible. He had stripped her of her dignity, virginity and modesty and she was not ready to face the world in that condition! She just did not know what to say or do. She was devastated.

As a matter of fact, she was so embarrassed that she did not know what to do. But one thing she did; she refused to leave Shechem's room. She supposed she had nowhere to go; how could she face her family after what had just happened to her! No way, she was not going anywhere she told Shechem. The young man then found himself between a rock and a hard place. Dinah turned into a dilemma right before his very eyes. At such turn of events, Shechem angry and confused went to speak with his dad about the unfolding situation.

Some Questions to Ponder

1. The young man Shechem had told Dinah how much he loved her. In your opinion, do you think that was true? Explain.
2. Eventually Shechem took Dinah to his home then into his room and there he carnally exploited her. What he did to Dinah is sometimes called date-rape; is it a common occurrence among the young people today? What could be the reasons for it and how can it be prevented or overcome? Discuss.
3. How would Dinah have handled the situation differently to avoid the rape ordeal from happening? What was she supposed to have done or not?
4. What do you as a young person learn from her story? What would be the right cause of action if someone were to approach you with sexual advances, are you supposed to hold them as your secrets or to report them to your superiors (seniors/parents or guardians)? Or does it depend on the context and circumstances? Explain
5. It has been claimed that in most cases the sexual advances come from relatives, neighbors or people well known to the young people. Why is this the case? What should be your response if such relatives or some other close persons were to

involve in such sexual advances or try to seduce you?

6. In some cases young people fear speaking out about sexual advances by relatives or even teachers because they think their parents or guardians would not believe them. Why is this the case? How can it be overcome?
7. Is rape a problem of the girl child only or does it apply to both sexes? Discuss.
8. How should a family respond to such a thing happening to their child? Discuss
9. In the situation of Dinah's rape, if we were to situate blame somewhere; who should we blame and why? Should we blame Dinah's parents since they did not know much of what went on in their daughter's life; Dinah herself for naivety claiming she brought rape on herself; Tina her friend who arranged the meeting between Dinah and Shechem; or Shechem for his behavior toward Dinah, or nobody at all considering what happened as an accident? Give reasons for your answers.

Shechem Confers With His Dad

It has been said that bad news travels fast, and so it did in this case. Within no time the wind of what Shechem had done to Dinah got out and spread in the whole city. Dinah banging on the door and her cries had attracted the attention of some of the Mayor's neighbors who soon learned of Dinah's rape and published the news throughout the city.

It happened when Shechem went to consult with his dad. One of the neighborhood girls, who had been attracted by Dinah's cries, and had been hiding nearby went to the door and knocked timidly. Dinah did not hear it at first, but heard the second knock yet ignored it all together. However, the girl tried the door and it opened. She sneaked inside asking,

"Who is there? Is everything all right in here?"

Dinah was still lying in bed crying when the girl got in and asked, "Who is there?" On hearing a girl's voice Dinah responded faintly,

"It is me." She said while still sobbing.

"Are you ok?" Enquired the girl moving toward the bed, but before Dinah could answer the girl somehow realized what must have happened. She then ran out of the room as quickly as she had come in. She left as though she was going to bring help, but she never returned.

However, she went and related the story to others and so they carried it to the whole city. The story of Dinah's defilement like her birth went around the city like wildfire. This was a small town and such news quickly found its way through the little town's community. Within no time almost everyone had heard the story of the rape of the newest girl in town by the richest young man thereat.

What a shameful thing it was for a person appearing to be a responsible young man to rape a girl he wanted to be friend! The means defeated the end in his case. Like has been said, an end is valueless if it's achieved through violating the principles of right moral conduct.

Some of the townspeople gathered in small groups chattering here and there, while other grimaced over the news that had by then filled their city. They tossed it to and fro in wonderment, even as some of them discredited Hamor and his son Shechem. They felt that the boy had crossed the line, and had transgressed good manners. They opined that his father needed to take some stern actions against him. But the most affected person was Tina. When she received this sad news; she almost fainted.

She ran into her bedroom and threw herself across the bed after shutting and latching the door. She then cried her head out. She could not believe that Shechem of all the people, could do such a thing; in fact, she could not even imagine it! How could he! It was contrary to whom she thought he was. Besides how would she face Dinah; what would she tell her? Would she continue to be her friend really? And if so, would Dinah ever forgive and trust her again; considering she recommended Shechem based on her presumption he was a gentleman? She wished this whole thing was just a rumor, but unfortunately it was the reality.

On the other hand when he got to his dad Shechem said, "Dad I have a rather difficult situation on my hands in which I need your help urgently."

"What is it this time son?" His dad asked.

"I happened to bring a girl into my room, but she has now refused to leave; what should I do?" He told his father.

"Who is the girl?" His father enquired.

"The daughter of the new Hebrew from Haran," Shechem responded.

"Oh, my! Why did you pick on her when there are so many beautiful Canaanite girls around?" Challenged his father.

"Father, she is pretty and very outgoing. I was attracted to her and told her how much I loved her." Shechem confided.

"So, you say she does not want to leave your room. Is it that she does not want to return to her home, and if so has she told you the reason why?" enquired the father.

"Not really, but I suppose it is because she may be embarrassed. Since I lay with her she has just been crying." Shechem answered.

"What did you do to her, did you hurt her in any way?" his father enquired further.

"No, I did nothing wrong to her; I brought her into the room and then we made love and she just started crying." Shechem explained.

"Girls just don't cry like that son; can you tell me exactly what happened and is this your first time with her or have you been with her another time?" His father enquired with a little seriousness.

Shechem then got into some detailed explanations to his dad, who finally asked him. "Son, if the lass does not want to return to her home, what do you think? Have you considered that you can marry her so that this whole thing can end amicably? Can you marry her?"

"Marry her, what do you mean dad? That is the last thing on my mind. Although she seems nice, I do not think I love her enough to marry her." He told his dad.

"But you loved her enough to sleep with her. Why can't you marry her?" The father asked sarcastically.

"I don't think I want to marry yet; it has nothing to do with this situation. Can you just tell me what to do with her right now and we can discuss those other things later?" Shechem answered.

"But you have humbled her and the logical thing to do now is to accept her as your wife so as not to complicate things; these Hebrew are new in our midst and we don't know how they will react if you let that girl return to her home. Don't you think it is time you settled down?" his father explained.

Dinah's situation came up in the backdrop of a case that had also involved Shechem with another girl named Luhtar. We already mentioned her earlier on. Hence, his father thought he needed to settle down by marrying Dinah and stopped running around with girls in wild escapades.

After a short time of further consultations with his dad, Shechem then agreed to marry Dinah presupposing it was his best option out. He then returned to his room to inform Dinah of his decision, but she rejected it and cried the more. She said she did not want any of such solutions. She wondered who told Shechem she wanted to be married.

Matrimonial connections were not to be made upon dereliction of Yahweh's principles of sobriety and virtuous living. Moreover, in her culture it was not upon her alone to decide she wanted to be married. Marriage was a big thing and could not be undertaken in unholy haste as was the situation facing her then. Its arrangements involved parental suggestions and guidance, since parents controlled the final decisions. Indeed, Parents even made choices for their children's mates in most cases. Of course arranged marriages were the order of the day then. How could she just announce her own marriage?

Furthermore, a cross-cultural marriage like the situation facing her then was out of question. Inter-marriages between the covenant people and non-covenant ones was forbidden. She had been taught that when a believer marries a non-believer, they would not live to that high standard that pleases Yahweh. The non-believer would eventually trap and seduce the believer, turning them away from fervently and vigorously living for and serving God. Those who were free to marry were admonished to do so, only in the household of faith or among the covenant people.

This is a solemn injunction which some young people and even those who had known Yahweh tended to ignore or forget, and inevitably destroyed themselves. Hence, Shechem bursting into the room and telling her that he was ready to marry her was adding insult to injury. Her main desire then was not marriage, but to have someone contact her family; especially her father.

Shechem's dad presupposed that marriage was their only way out of that predicament for his son. However, it has been observed that marriages entered into on the basis of reasons other than personal full commitment to live with each other are bound to fail. Without such a commitment there is no dynamism that will let and urge the couple to care for, or treat each other as we would want to be treated. That is the reason people who marry without full personal commitment to their spouses, simply because of some circumstances like unplanned pregnancy or having had sexual intercourse, will always have untold troubles and heartaches. Yet that seemed to have been the only solution to the young man's family.

Dinah's Family Contacted

Shechem's family deliberated on the unfolding events and then agreed that the girl's family had to be informed immediately of the situation at hand and their decision on it. And so, Shechem and his dad went to see the girl's family. Jacob welcomed them into his homestead as though he had not heard the bad news. Thus, sitting across from them he forced a smile even as he looked at his sons.

Then Shechem's dad told Jacob and his sons: "My son Shechem really loves Dinah. Please let him marry her. As a matter of fact, let us arrange other marriages, too. You give us your daughters for our sons, and we will give you our daughters for your sons. Live among us freely; the land is big enough and open to you too! Feel free to move about until you find the property you want; then buy it and settle down here and trade with us."

And his son added, "Do this favor for me, and I'll give whatever you want. Ask anything of me, no matter how expensive or difficult and I'll do it; just let me marry Dinah."

He spoke hiding the exact details of what he had done to her earlier, but the news had already reached Jacob and his family. Oh, what a situation this young man brought his parents into!

On receiving the news of Dinah's rape ordeal, her dad was not amused; he grew pale with fury and was dumbfounded. Meanwhile, his sons had just returned home from the pastures and as soon as they heard that their sister had been raped; they were not amused either. They got furious and were displeased that Shechem had done such a disgraceful and disrespectful thing to their sister. It was a sign of his disrespect not only for her, but for their whole family and they loathed it.

In their view, nothing was more disgraceful to any woman than rape. They knew that every woman has a right to be consulted in regards to sexual engagements. Forced sexual intercourse is a violation of any person's dignity and rights, especially a woman's. It is debasing the woman's dignity and worth, and so they secretly vowed to revenge.

They were not going to tolerate it happening to their very own beloved sister. If left like that it might happen to someone else so they reasoned. They did not consider sexual rights to be a preserve of men, more so rich and powerful men. Women as equal, though different, partners of men have the same rights too. Women's rights are as much human rights as are the men's. They thereby agreed that something drastic had to be done to the young man. But since the young man was the mayor's son, they figured out that if they waited for justice from the city courts then it was a long way coming.

Furthermore, there seemed to be no prescribed penalty or punishment for male sexual transgressors like Shechem in their society. But they so badly wanted justice, or simply put they wanted to get even with him. Though new in that city, they vowed not to let such a heinous act committed against their own go unpunished. And hence, secretly they kept scheming.

Then a few weeks later Simeon and Levi, Dinah's brothers from the same mother led a bloody revenge attack against the city. They killed the rapist young man and his father and all the city's male inhabitants. They then plundered the city taking away women and children and animals. It was a bloody revenge like nothing ever seen or heard of in that place. All brought about just by a careless act of one young man!

This bespeaks that one person's careless act can always result into great catastrophes on others not even associated with the original act.

Nonetheless, Dinah lost her virginity forever. Her story ends that her brothers took her away from the young man's house, but she was never the same. A raped victim never remains the same; they lose something about them. That is what happened to Dinah. She was violated, dishonored and shamed; having been taken advantage of by a young man she had just met and would have wanted to know further. As wonderful as was the beginning of her history, with all the neighborhood celebrations; its end was not only tragic but traumatic too.

Some Questions to Ponder

1. After her rape ordeal Dinah seemed to have lost her usual self-confidence; why do you think that was the case?
2. Why did Dinah refuse to come out of Shechem's room? Was it guilt or shame or both, or just confusion as to what exactly had happened to her? Explain

3. We find that the consequence of this young man's action was very devastating to his family and the city as a whole. Can you give some examples of situations where young people have gotten their families into problems by their irresponsible behaviors that may not necessarily be sexual? What do we learn from such?
4. When the young man Shechem raped Dinah, his father eventually began talking about marriage; should marriage be the next best alternative for young people who have been sexually misused or abused? Give reasons for your answers.
5. Supposing Shechem and Dinah went ahead and got married from the arrangement the boy's father was pushing for; do you think they would have lived happily ever after, having one of the best marriages? Explain your answer.
6. When Shechem's dad told him to marry Dinah he commented that he did not love her enough to marry her. What does this tell us? Is this a common attitude with both sexes; loving people just for what you can get without real regards to their person?
7. Are there different levels of love; some just for using people to deriving pleasures from them;

while another level for commitment to long term relationships?

Other Examples Within this Context

The unfortunate fact is that Dinah's story is not an isolated case. Rape is a prevalent occurrence even today. Indeed, even in what appears to be normal relationships. And it is sad that in such budding friendships, most young men always pressurize or force girls into having sex with them against the girls' consciences. Some of them claim that the girls are theirs and they can do whatever they like with them. Yet those who hide behind love as the reason for their sleeping with their girlfriends, claim they do so to prove if the girls really love them. Yet, shortly later, most of those boys dump those girls. How unfortunate but common.

Nonetheless, in some cases even some girls themselves initiate such sexual involvements with men or boys, because they feel reassured of love and acceptance through yielding to sex. That was what we observed with the Canaanite girls. But it is a flawed notion, since such girls derive their worth from being exploited or misused.

In other words, without using them those who purport to love or want them would not! Their so-called love is pegged on their getting free access to the girls' bodies. If the girls refuse with their treasures, those boys will walk off to other women; proving that there was no love in the first place. So are the girls really loved, or this is just about sex?

A case example here was that of a young man who threatened his girlfriend with breakup if she could not give him sex. Without much thought the girl presumed it was normal for boys to behave that way. She did not realize that that was manipulation that could eventually lead to her exploitation. Yet, because of emotional dependency or attachment she had developed over the said young man, she gave in to having sex with him. However, a few weeks later he dumped her. The girl was devastated.

She was afraid of losing him in the first place and gave in to having sex with him presuming she was giving him love so as to retain him. But that trick did not work; she lost him without any explanations. Immediately he had sex with her, he lost the curiosity and appreciation for her. In his mind he was wondering how many other young men must have been sleeping with her. He eventually left her bewildered.

The girl wanted friendship and love, but not necessarily sex. However, the young man like many others was only keen on sex and therein lies the difference. The girl later confessed that she desperately wanted her boyfriend to love and affirm her; just for who she was and not necessarily for what she could give him. That is, she wanted *unconditional* love; unfortunately, she was promised it on *condition* that she gave sex first! Then she gave in to that sexual intercourse presuming their love would blossom. But that was a presumption with no guarantee. She was left without an explanation.

Obviously, unconditional love promised on condition of what one can give is not unconditional love. That is the reason wisdom has it that anyone promising you love on condition of sex is not the right friend to pursue further relationships with. Dinah must have learnt that fact too late to be of any help to her.

However, it is not only the young women who are taken advantage of these days; even the older ones fall victims to some unscrupulous men. There is a case of a mature lady who had a crush on ("fell in love" with) a work mate at a job training facility in another city. She became obsessed with him and related how they used to talk several times a day.

Especially, the guy called to convey his love for her and whenever he did not, the lady called him. They could talk even for about two hours over the phone. They lived in different cities then and mostly met on weekends. The irony of their relationship was that the lady was a "born-again" Christian while the man was not, though the girl claimed he was nicer than most Christians she knew.

The lady shared the news of her new found love with her pastor, who cautioned her against a relationship not based on the same faith principles. But she somehow felt it was God's Will for her to have that man in her life. She wanted him to love her so bad that she was not ready to listen to anyone. With that she rejected wisdom from Nancie and William Carmichael, and Dr. Timothy Boyd; who in their book *That Man*[1], say and I paraphrase: *when all we are after is to be loved then we will eventually be disappointed because those we project on to love us are also looking for love.*

Accordingly, that is where this lady lost it; she was just out looking for someone to love her for herself. The whole thing was just about her and not even the lover. When the church pointed out such facts, telling her she

---

[1] *That Man;* William Carmichael, Nancie Carmichael and Timothy Boyd: Thomas Nelson Inc. 1988

was approaching that whole matter from a wrong perspective; she quit the church claiming they were simply jealous of her new found love. Indeed, she claimed that was why they were intruding into her private affairs.

Thereafter, she frequented the young man's city, and there were signs they might have become sexually intimate even though she denied it. But it was reported that they sometimes even spent nights together. Shortly afterwards, they went on a vacation overseas to Europe; just the two of them with the man intending to propose to her. But something terrible happened out there.

Their vacation ended abruptly before the due date and they returned home on different flights to the surprise of many. Things were never the same for them after that. The lady was hurt, and was always angry at the man. She became disillusioned about their love. But her 'boyfriend' began seeing other women in disregard to the feelings of his "faithful Christian" girlfriend.

That infuriated the lady even the more, and eventually their relationship totally disintegrated and fell apart. The man claimed that the girl was trying to control him, while the girl asserted that the young man was unfaithful liar who did not care about her in any way. However, some of their friends rumored that the guy had told a friend how lousy the girl was in love making and that he was not interested in her any more. He sampled and categorized her and then broke her heart, and walked off to conqueror other unsuspecting women!

The lady's self-worth was crushed. It was reported she had confided in a friend that his boyfriend had betrayed her when they went to Europe. She claimed to have caught him in bed with another woman. Both their claims could not be verified, but definitely something went wrong between them.

She was lured, toured and dumped; and that is where it hurts even the most. Moreover, having given yourself wholeheartedly to someone and your relationship ends unceremoniously like that; it hurts, and it may inhibit your ability to love freely in the future. Or if you do, the depth of your passion would be lacking. That is one of the reasons there are many problems with relationships, most of which tend towards emptiness and loneliness.

Alarmingly, the frequency with which such heart rending cases occur is unfathomable. But that is because most young people tend to brush aside such warnings. They presume that such incidences can never happen to them because they are in love. Yet, if it has happened to others it can happen to anyone; love is no deterrent. Even more devastating is the myth of sex first and love after. It is putting the cart before the horse. Like has been said, those who crowd divorce courts today once thought the same. They discovered so late that sex first does not make you love happily ever after.

Love at First Sight (Falling in Love)

When the lady in in the story above saw the guy at that training workshop, she had a crush on him and her world was turned upside down. This happened as a result of the notion called falling in love. It is commonly expressed by those who believe they have somehow *stumbled* upon someone they love. Yet such mindless falling in love, in most cases, turn out to be a source of great problems when the concerned persons carry on with it. Why? Because such folks equate the intensity of their feelings with the realities they expect from those others. But they are wrong because feelings change as frequently as the days go by. Yet, such people seemingly do not anticipate any of such changes and thereby get frustrated when reality hits home.

Commonly, love finds its essence in relationships as an integral part of them. It is supposed to be the bedrock of any such relationships. Yet honestly no one ever falls into a relationship. This then is the irony; one cannot fall into a relationship, yet can fall in love! Nonetheless, that is a misconception. How does it happen that one can fall in love yet not in a relationship? Is it true? Clearly, people cannot fall into a relationship because a relationship or even love, is never automatic. They take time to develop and then have to be cultivated, worked on and built by discreet nurturing. There are no relationships at first sight as people often claim with love.

Thus, the falling in love notion is simply a convolution of people's instant emotional reactions to stimuli arising from their encounters with others. It is the instantaneous buildup of exciting imaginary feelings of suspense, and wonderment they imagine they can derive from those they encounter. Mostly, more so if they were to indulge in sex with them. But the reality is quite different from and independent of all such instantaneous feelings of suspense. That is why such relationships don't last; more so when the involved individuals begin to face life realities.

Researchers have found out that falling in love is normally followed by falling out of it. That means, when people fall in love; they will eventually fall out of it if they do nothing to secure their relationships. It has been referred to as an *ignis fatuus*; a fire of straw that makes a bright blaze, but soon goes out. Does this mean we should ignore our feelings towards others? Of course not, but we should respond to and channel them appropriately without giving them unnecessary focus. We should allow them adequate time to prove they are indeed, love and not just the mere urge for coition. But people mostly never do that! They let their feelings loose and rush headlong into situations without much considerations.

Nonetheless, there are people who have fallen in love and later worked out their relationships to thriving ones. But note my statement that they worked out things to steer them into a thriving relationship not just feelings of love. Any so-called love where feeling is the basis and no adjustments are made for each other will never become a wholesome relationship. That is what falling in love is; a feeling saturated involvement in which people emphasize the intensity of their feelings, at the expense of concrete factors that matter to every relationship.

Furthermore, those who fall in love don't consider the maxim 'opposites attract'. By being instantly attracted to each other, it might be that you are oddly opposites to each other like the North and South poles of the magnetic fields. Thereafter, when their emotional flares cool down, and their feelings begin to twist and distort into uncertainty; they will not be able to stand each other.

Dr. Paul A Cedar in his book, *Becoming a Lover* [2] says that falling out of love simply means that the emotional feelings for the other person have been eroded and disappeared. He states that the warm feelings or emotions many people often exhibit toward others and confuse to be love are actually not love. Such people misunderstand love by identifying it only as an emotion or feeling, whereas true love is an act of the will. And such a love is in the power of everyone's choice. He argues that if love was merely something one would unintentionally "fall in", then God would not command us to love others!

A.W. Tozer one of the profound Christian Pastors by the turn of the century, added that the love God commands is not the love of feelings, but rather of willing. He calls it the willed tendency of the heart. That is, thoughtfully and by deliberate action of the will we are to choose to love others. He calls 'falling in love' the love of feelings which brings feelings of love that come and go, rise and fall, flare up and disappear very much as does the

---

[2] *Becoming a Lover*, Paul A Ceder: Tyndale House Publishers, 1978

weather. Clearly, according to him, no one can depend on such a "love".

Dr. James Dobson, the known American Child psychologist, also adds his voice to this issue by stating that falling in love is a distorted concept of romantic love. It a confusion of the real thing with infatuation. He says that in it emotions are unleashed at first sight, but such emotions do not constitute love. They are feelings that are temporary and differ from love in that they are merely emotions, which place emphasis on the one feeling them rather than on the object of love. Besides, they are selfish and are motivated by desire for self-gratification.

That is one of the reasons falling in love does not build or result into long term relationships. It rests on the foundation of selfishness. Experts in these matters have found out that falling in love is usually or mostly about, or tends toward sexual love and not necessarily relationships. That is, falling in love is more about sexual copulation than just pure relationships.

Hence, those who fall in love are in essence, merely functioning on the premise of sexual engagements. That is, falling in love works only for and towards one thing, "sexual intercourse". Yet relationships are known to involve a multitude of other factors that make them stable beyond just having sex.

DeVern Fromke, a fine longtime gospel minister, on his part says that the term falling in love is a true description of the nature or kind of the love being spoken of. It is indeed, a love that has fallen from or falling short of God's high standard. He says that when love falls from God's high standard, it becomes lust and uncontrollable passion which works only towards individual's self-gratification. He points out that the more tragic realization is how love has fallen even in the church!

He then explains that this 'falling in love' notion implies some two false impressions about love. First, that love is some sort of a trap that one can fall into and then becomes a hopeless, helpless victim who cannot control or even extricate him or herself. Second, that love is some irresistible force like a magnetic pull that overcomes one at the sight of another, forcing them to love those they encounter regardless of conditions or circumstances (w*apende wasipende* [3]).

Thus, if someone were to tell you; "I could not help falling in love with you." It should be clear to you that they do not have control over themselves. Anyone who falls in love will soon or later fall out of it. Thus, you

---

[3] *Wapende wasipende*, is a Swahili expression which translates to whether they like it or not

should not accept relationships with people who seemingly cannot control themselves. They will run off with someone else, leaving you heartbroken claiming that love forced them to.

For instance, I once read of a man who told his bride as they were signing their marriage contract that theirs was to be a free and open arrangement. They were not to bind each other, in case they happened to find other lovers they would have liked to try out. They were free to pursue them too, nothing hindering. Seemingly, he had bought into the notions of those who presume that true lovers give each other permission to do whatever they wished. But it is debatable if such a philosophy is a sign of true love or just liberalism.

This guy's commitment to his so-called bride was questionable from the start. He was only keen at making provisions for himself in case his longings were unfulfilled in that marriage. And surprisingly it was reported that he did not even last one year in that marriage. Shortly afterwards, he ran off with another woman in the name of love; how tragic!

Another example here involved Becky Gwanda, and Noe Kanana. They 'fell in love' after Becky led him to the Lord. To her joy she set out to help him spiritually by instructing him in God's word. She did not consider that an attraction might develop between them, because she was only doing God's work of nurturing the new believer.

However, unsuspectingly and inadvertently an attraction and a fondness developed between them as they spent time together. Not long later, they madly fell in love, and got married in an elaborate wedding ceremony. But after a year or so, their so-called marriage fell apart. They got into loggerheads with each other ending in their marriage hitting a rock bottom.

Their emotions cooled off and they discovered that they did not really love each other. In fact, they were then seeing things differently. They had presumed they were in such deep love that they could hardly live without each other. But then they realized they did not want to be near each other. What a contrast! It dawned on them that their love was but superficial.

Mr. Kanana became bitter, claiming that Becky had trapped him in a marriage he did not even want in the first place. He renounced his faith in God and disclaimed ever having confessed Jesus Christ as his savoir. He had by then stopped going to church and did not want anything to do with Christians. Becky herself felt like she was in a bad dream. She did not understand how things could turn out like that, yet she loved the Lord. She was wondering what she did wrong.

Anyway, she sought marriage counselling hoping to change things around. But Joe was not interested and eventually their marriage ended just like that. They went their separate ways disillusioned and heartbroken.

From these cases we learn that the deepest and most permanent form of love, is that which has been built over time. There is no need to rush love, you have the whole of your life ahead of you. Young people should take their sweet time; there is no need to hurry love.

The foundation to build your life-long relationship on must be a love that has grown, firmly laid and built with sanctity in character enswathed. This means, it is important to understand that long term relationships cannot be built on the mere feelings at first sight. Feelings change daily and are not enough to sustain a life-long relationship. That is why the love between any two people wanting to deepen their relationship must be commitment-driven rather than emotions or feelings-driven.

Unfortunately, some young people even today have bought into the myth that what, or how they feel is what is important. But they should be cautioned that even those who crowd the divorce courts today, bitter and disillusioned, were once quite in love with each other as they may feel they are. But they failed to consider that with time, their *feelings* would change.

Hence, feelings as good as they may be should not be the basis on which to build your relationship. You will do yourself a favor by not measuring love by emotions exhibit towards you, especially on your first encounter.

A person is not exactly that smile you see on the first encounter. Who they really are is quite different. Do not assume you know people simply because of their smiles. The real person is not the sweet smile they flash at you on your first encounter. Do not even measured their so-called love by the number of times they call you to say they love you. True love is not just a verbalized expression of "I love you". What they are saying to you they might be telling someone else; hence, it should not be your yardstick for measuring love. True love is exhibited in acts of kindness, honor, respect and understanding involving self-control that values others.

Another thing that will keep you going strong in your love is respect. If you want others to value and respect you; do so yourself. Begin by respecting yourself: your body, your image and everything you stand for. Then set some limits and boundaries for yourself; more so, from God's word and live within them. This is so important because worthwhile living is possible, but only within the bounds of some concrete and good moral values enshrined on God's stipulations.

Television commentator Ted Koppel said, "There is harmony and inner peace to be found in following a moral compass that points in the same direction regardless of fashion or trend." Everyone needs this moral compass, which God and His word is to us. Therefore, be sensible and seek long term commitment before giving yourself to anyone. Remember that a life without values (limits) is a valueless life, and yet there is no value-free living anywhere whether in the public or in private.

Questions to Ponder

1. In one of the case examples above featuring Joe Kanana and Becky Gwanda, toward the end we read Joe's claim that Becky trapped him in a marriage he did not want in the first place! The question then arises as to what was he after in Becky's life if he did not want marriage? Discuss. Is this common?
2. The narrative ends that their marriage ended just like that. They went their separate ways disillusioned and hurt. Do you think they were equally hurt? Discuss
3. When Shechem came looking for Dinah, he claimed to have been struck by her beauty. In other words he fell in love with her at first sight. What

do you think of love at first sight? Discuss cons and pro giving examples if any

Some Common Reasons for Premarital Sex

Peer Pressure from notions like everyone is doing it, is one of the reasons people plunge into premarital sex. The line most of the young people seem to hear a lot is that everyone is doing it. All their friends seemingly are engaged in it in one way or the other and they seem to be the only ones oddly left out. But that is a great hype, not everyone is doing it. There are many others out there, who have taken the vow of purity and refuse to indulge themselves in such fleeting pleasures.

Hence, you are not alone. But these are pressures piled on us every day via the media - the television, movies, books, magazines and so forth to make us conform to the new societal standards. They are portrayed to entice one to join the bandwagon of the supposed joys of such involvements, otherwise they may suffer what has been called the FOMO – *Fear of Missing Out*.

It cannot be stressed enough the role the music and videos have recently played in this phenomenon, polluting people's minds about sex and love, and the opposite gender or even same gender involvements. And even the print media is not left behind. To underscore how widespread this is; I once read some misconstrued statements about sexology in one of the magazines, which I cannot quite remember. But I can remember the lines, which went something like:

> Today to fully explore your sexuality is as healthy as it is fun. The exploration begins as you choose a variety of partners (slim, fat, short, tall etc.), which is what makes sexual intercourse more fun. No one needs to say no to such experiences. Men and women have delighted themselves in them over the years and they can all testify to the fact of the pleasures they derived from such. If you are serious about getting wonderful personal sexual experiences, then you must reject guilt, embarrassments and the social stigma normally attached to (associated with) love making. With this you will find

out why millions of people are sexually liberated today.

At face value one is bound to presume that those who practice the so-called free sex are liberated, but that is not necessarily the case. Those are just innuendos. The millions of people portrayed in that article as liberated sexually are in fact sexually disillusioned! That is an open secret they will never let you into. Most of such people don't have any specific solid and true relationships.

They are just fumbling around from one misstep to another searching for what they have already destroyed by their inauthentic lifestyles. Theirs is more of a sex hunt partnership rather than true mutual relationships of strength and unity of hearts. That which unites the involved in the fondness of being. But such folks are ignorant of this true meaning of dignified sexual enjoyment, because they perpetually pursue it by methods that plunge them into heartaches and misery on the account of their affinity to promiscuity.

The magazine spoke of how to begin your sexual exploration, but in reality that is a misuse of terms. Experts have found out that sexual intercourse is more of a programming than an exploration. As one engages in sex, they get programmed with their mate's and even their own responses and actions. Hence, it is false to insinuate that sexual exploration or experimentations enhance one's sexual enjoyment.

There is also the line, which read that sex is more fun with a variety of partners. This one is also false even though it is a popular widespread misconception they toss around to motivate people into experimentation with a variety of partners. Former President of Antioch College, Horace Mann, said that those who have never subdued an impulse in obedience to a principle talk in vain of happiness or fun. This is because the experts have observed that free or casual sex does more harm than good. Seeking of sexual enjoyment in diversity not only ensures disappointments, but it also generates discord.

Wherever such an approach is espoused, there is always some kind of violence lurking in the shadows. Sex and violence become part culture of such a lifestyle. It ultimately leads to self-hate, guilt, loneliness, sense of worthlessness, dissatisfaction with life and overwhelmed feelings; especially from the ladies' point of view. That then negatively impacts the person's emotional, social and even physical wellbeing.

Research has recently found out that a woman's sexual enjoyment increases with one person; when she is focused on one person, who cares deeply about her rather than with many individuals who can simply fulfill her immediate sexual urges. To every woman, a one-on-one deeply secure relationship is of greater value, giving her satisfaction than a thousand loose affiliations. Such a relationship then becomes her center (fort) of existence; generating hope, aspirations and appreciation, mutual respect and personal enrichment. This is because her sexuality is tied to her persona that tends toward loyalty, accountability, support, full commitment and nurture. Yet there is no loyalty, accountability, commitment, nurture, security and support with multiple sexual partners.

This bespeaks that love to a woman is more than just sex, because her feminine constitution demands a deeper, closer and tighter relationship than a mere sexual act. Relationship to her is based on a holistic approach to her persona not just on sex. That is why a woman is known to be safer and more fulfilled in a one on one intimate relationship than with a crowd or with a number of different guys.

Every woman has dreams and yearnings, desiring someone she enjoys being with; an individual she can fully open up to and share herself with. Someone she can share her hopes, dreams and even fears with without being misunderstood or judged. Clearly, she is after a person she can trust and be sincerely frank with; who can deeply care for her and she too can care for. That person who can treat her as special, because she really is both unique and special.

Yet, those who involve with many men are not in any way happier than those who don't. They have simply bought into the contemporary sway of trying to figure out who amongst the many men best suits them. Because in reality, every woman is after intimacy only with one person who can become a special asset to her in terms of investing in and enriching her person. It is that individual who needs and cherishes her more than the sex she can provide. That is the one who can lead her into a true intimacy that will then give her security, confidence and fulfilment.

Thus, secure and confident women are those who are valued and cherished not by several men, but by that one special person in their lives. How then can free-sex involving many partners, a practice that breeds jealousy, hurts and such negative emotions be considered fun! There is nothing loving in involving sexually with several people in the name of love! It is a hit-and-miss approach that targets love, but through unreasonable affairs that always leave people hurt.

Although notions that promiscuity is fun are supported and promoted by legions of sexually oriented mass media culture of today; promiscuity does not lead to a life of fun. Dr. I. Emery Breitner studied some eighty-eight promiscuous persons whom he termed as "love addicts"[4]. He observed that among other things they are mostly *lonely* souls looking for approval (acceptance) from others and an attachment to them by using sex. Yet it is an attachment that never is, as it utterly eludes them.

The magazine went further saying that when your conscience pricks you with guilt about wrong sexual involvements, then that is simply an embarrassment from social stigma. But the truth be told; anyone can and will experience such awful feelings as long as they undertake sexual acts wrongfully. It does not matter whether they subscribe to the so-called social stigma or not.

The statements of this magazine focused so much on the subjective aspect of life: the feelings, experiences, and pleasures, but not on the actual results of the purported involvements. They fail to reveal that every human action has its consequences. Typically, wrongful sexual involvements will always result in wrong or negative consequences, whether the person believes it or not. This has got nothing to do with belief, but actions that produce the consequences.

The good Book puts it thus; don't be misled—you cannot mock the justice of God. You will always harvest what you plant. Those who live only to satisfy their own

---

[4] "Love Addicts", Parade, April 1, 1973, p.9.

sinful nature will harvest decay and death from that sinful nature.

Another translation of the good Book says it slightly differently but the same message: Make no mistake about this: You can never make a fool out of God (who put the laws of morality in effect. You may deny, disbelieve or even ignore them) for whatever you plant is what you'll harvest. If you plant in the soil of your corrupt (fleshly) nature, you will harvest destruction.

That is, the consequences of carnal sexual escapades that many people presume to be fun, lead to destruction of relational intimacy. It destroys the peace, love and joy that relationships are supposed to give people. Eventually the relationship itself is destroyed. What these people (the promiscuous) try to build is destroyed by the very means they employ in doing so, because they reject God' moral stipulations.

Indeed, people who ignore the time-tested wisdom of life and take themselves to the edge of morality often go overboard and their lives never remain the same. In the good Book, such a person is referred to as unwise builder, whose relationships (edifice) don't stand the tests of time. In other words, in life short cuts don't pay dividends in the long run. If you cut corners now in your youth be sure that eventually the reality of your actions will catch up with you later.

The statements of that magazine viewed from a proper context, were simply innuendoes meant to lure the unsuspecting persons into the camp of the sexually disillusioned. Clearly, those who play with sex; treating it lightly, often get hurt even though they may go around pretending they are happy.

2. The next common reason young people involve in illicit sex is for **experience** sake, or to discover how it feels. Like Adam and Eve they just want to taste and judge for themselves how it feels. But they should be cautioned that hedonism is not one of the pillars to build a strong and lasting relationship on. It is simply a craving for an experience against morality encouraged by unbelief in God's sound prohibitions against such indulgences. Many are they, who seek the pleasurable experience that is supposedly derivable from sexual involvements. But such feelings will always elude them, because they seek them wrongfully.

Like has been pointed out sex affects the whole person: the spirit, soul and body and that makes it difficult for those who are out only for the feeling to readily register such. To plunge into it so as to have such feelings would require many of such involvements, yet at the end of it all remaining with no specific feelings registered. To score this point Y. N. Harari writes, and I quote:

If I identify happiness with fleeting pleasant sensations, and crave to experience more and more of them, I have no choice but to pursue them constantly. When I finally get them they quickly disappear and because the memory of the mere past pleasures will not satisfy me, I have to start all over again. Even if I continue this pursuit for decades, it will never bring me any lasting achievement; on the contrary, the more I crave these pleasant sensations, the more stressed and dissatisfied I will become.[5]

Dwight Small, a refined author and marriage counselor of some time ago said that sexual infidelity can never lead to sexual fulfilment of any kind, or to any satisfaction at all since it is sexuality without true mutuality. He calls it a fraud, and an empty exercise that fails to communicate the true values for which sex was given. Thus, every illicit sexual activity will not give anyone the desired feelings, since it is the treading underfoot of the virtuous principles of Yahweh by the personal dictates of fleeting passions.

---

[5] Yuval Noah Harari, *Homo Deus A Brief History Of Tomorrow*, HarperCollins Publishers, 195 Broadway, NY 10007, 2017 pg 42.

3.   **Curiosity** is another reason for ill-timed sexual involvements. This is about those out to try it to find out what this sex matter is all about. It is like they want to venture into a voyage of discovery to find out that mysterious draw about it that beckons their hearts and affections.

This is tremendously contributed to by the media; much more, the music videos of today. Music on television has played a dangerous role in oversexualizing the minds of people to the point where sexual love has no meaningful value. It is portrayed just as a recreational element of people's lives meant to give them good feelings. It is essentially rendered valueless. Yet, studies on sexology have shown that value based sexual love is what adds worth to the involved persons. Whereas, the hit-and-run type of approaches to love has no limit once people get started down that road. Many of them then get so caught up in it to the point that they end up having no control of themselves.

In fact, today there are even those so-called sex addicts in whom the curiosity has turned into a curse of uncontrolled insatiable passionate desires. They are those who carry licentiousness and gratification of their fleshly appetites too far. Yet, it is an open secret that licentious living is vain delight and a fleeting existence that results in emotional instabilities of every kinds. That is because when we say yes to what God has forbidden; then we are setting sail for the dangerous harbors of sin, shame and misery. There, our peace, joy and self-respect are destroyed and totally wiped out leaving us with self-loathing and hopelessness.

4. Others claim that ill-sexual engagement is natural and a healthy response to sexual feelings and a means to:
- ❖ Having good times and enjoying their God given rights, – however, every God given right has its place and bounds of expressions
- ❖ Expressing their love, – this is a convolution of terms as sex should be the platform where love reaches its highest peak; the culmination of love and not just its mere expression
- ❖ Fulfilling the nature's call upon their desires – yet those living by their natural dictates are living within the *Adamic sphere of existence*, which is a fallen state that is without (short of) Yahweh's glory
- ❖ Killing loneliness or boredom – these dispositions are still in the realm of feelings and emotions that cannot be opiated by sex alone. Sex does not cure boredom or loneliness.

Necessity for Premarital Sexual Abstinence

On the conservative front, prohibiting premarital sexual involvements is for the youths' good despite the fact that they never realize it then. Experts have come up with some reasons as to why premarital sex should be avoided, especially the free unattached sexual lifestyle.

1. It **leads to less happy marriages**. When one engages in sex before marriage, they will be prone to compare and contrast the same when they get into their marriage. This means they are more likely to lose sexual enthusiasm, if things do not measure up to their past sexual experiences. That will eventually result in their being unfulfilled and they will end up unhappy in their marriages. This non-fulfilment may then lead them into unfaithfulness as they try to look for it outside their marriage.

This could also be because most people with premarital sexual experiences seem programmed to continue the same life style. It is normally stated: once a cheat always a cheat. This is explained by researchers Blumstein and Schwartz who say, "People who have had premarital sexual intercourse are likely to have extramarital intercourse or easily involve sexually with someone not their spouse."

That is so because it is a character they developed outside marriage, but which they carried over into it trying to relive their past experiences. Obviously everyone carries with them their measures of trust and betrayals wherever they go. And marriage is no exception; people get into marriage with all sorts of baggage. That is, if you were a liar or what-have-you; you will still be the same person in your marriage.

A person's character, as the reflections of his or her soul, remains the same until altered by a greater force impressing on it externally. It is built slowly from habits by degrees, but stays on longer by usage according to that which flirts upon it. Hence, when people form a flirtatious habit before marriage, nothing will change them; they will continue to be the same in their married life. Marriage itself, as a life station, does not cure or change people's character; it does not stop roving eyes and philandering heart. You will always be who you brought into your marriage in the first place.

That is why young people are advised to abstain from premarital sex; it is about their future. It is their protection from a future dull and unfulfilling marriage, arising from previous experiences of betrayals and breakups.

2.　　It **brings strains to marriages**. Sometimes this is not so obvious, but it is the number one cause of suspicions and uneasiness in marriages. People who have been sleeping around before marriage usually tend to mistrust each other, especially in how closely or freely they talk to or relate with other people, even workmates. They always imagine that others could be seducing they spouses, and consequently they somehow become unduly suspicious.

In fact, some of such people can be very mean and jealous. They dread their spouses talking freely to or laughing with other people. They feel threatened and uneasy when their spouses are not under their watchful eyes. They do not know what those spouses could up to! They always imagine bad things of their spouse; wondering if they could be seeing other people. This makes them mistrust others, who freely talk to or associate with their spouses.

Progressively, they end up mistrusting each other in their marriages and that then pushes them apart. Eventually romance dies and if they do not resolve their problems early enough; their marriage may end up breaking.

3. It becomes **the basis of some spousal abuses and control**, eventually leading to infidelity. A number of people who have had premarital sexual experiences tend to be manipulative in their later relationships. They tend to want to control every facet of their love life, so much so that their mates have to totally yield to their dictates and demands on how that relationship should go. They presume they are the ones who know what is best for their marriages. Yet this they do simply for themselves, as a precaution to prevent a repeat of some of the unfavorable results from their previous experiences. There is something they are fearing, which they are then projecting onto their spouses.

Some of such people then use sex as a weapon for demanding and controlling things in their relationships. Especially, the ladies are prone to this thereby easily hurting their husbands in the process. Yet, when that is done and it appears that sex is being rationed in his marriage; the man will opt to shop for it elsewhere ending up in infidelity. The same is true of women who do not get their conjugal rights in their marriages. They also end up gravitating toward infidelity, although theirs begins much secretively. Eventually, such a lifestyle plunges them into unbearable rivalry and competitions that will finally break up their marriage.

4. It **may force one into marrying someone who is not right for them, or even marry at the wrong time**. A case example here happened to Mwajuma Achupa, who got pregnant by one of her brother's friends. This young man frequented their home and somehow they got used to one another. Then one thing led to another and before they knew it, the girl was pregnant. The two families then met and resolved that the youths had to marry, yet it had not even crossed their minds when they were having sex. To them it was only a matter of exploiting it for fun, as those infatuated with what they had access to.

They were neither ready for, nor even thinking about marriage. The young man had no steady source of income. He was looking to his father's support while the lady had just finished college. They found themselves forced into marriage, unplanned. Yet, even the parents forcing them to marry did not correct the wrong already done. In any case, the parents only opted for this as a means of maintaining a good face in the society, but with the least interest of the two young people at heart.

5. **Couples with premarital experiences are likely to be less satisfied with their married sex life because of prior experiences conflicting programming.** Josh McDowell, one of the American Christian apologists, in his book *Sex why Wait* [6] says as he quotes Dr. Gerhard Dirks that sex is programming. He states that when a woman has intercourse with a man, the man programs her a certain way. She is programmed to respond visually, audibly and mechanically to certain sets of actions.

If she is programmed by many men before marriage then when she settles down for marriage, she will not respond totally to the programming of her husband. This is due to the conflicting programming of her past experiences.

Hence, they will not derive much sexual enjoyment from each other. Especially to the woman, sex will just be one of her routine duties to be fulfilled and be done with quickly. This will make her presume that either her husband does not know how to satisfy her sexually, or that sex is generally boring which may not be the case.

---

[6] *Why Wait*, Josh McDowell: Thomas Nelson Publishers, Nashville, 1987

To avoid such quandary of experiences, Dr. McDowell concludes; it is, therefore, best for two people to wait for marriage so they can be programmed together for maximum sexual satisfaction. That is one of the reasons young people are advised against sexual involvements before marriage. Dr. McDowell sums it that "Sex at the right time, with the right person, in the right relationship is found to be so incredibly perfect."

Restoration

For the many young people who may not have been sexually exploited or abused, and have read Dinah's story; it is not too late to take a moral and an appropriate stand on this matter. Yet, even those who may have gone the way of Dinah, whether rape or consensual sexual involvements, there is always a new beginning. You can start afresh with God. His word is replete with people who opted to return to Him and made it right.

Nothing is wrong in your returning to the Lord, if indeed you have strayed away from Him. It is one of the best moves you can take when life tries to box you up. The Lord of mercy is anticipating your knock at His door of grace. Actually, falling into sexual sin or being abused is not an ultimate failure with God, but refusing to take remedial action after the ordeal is.

Remember God's grace is sufficiently available to all people at all times for all that they may need including restorations. This is the picture we observed in the case of Dinah when her brothers finally took her away from Shechem's house. She had been defiled and traditionally she was unfit to rejoin her family. Such a one was then only fit to be stoned publicly to death or cast away from the community forever. But Dinah found love and grace from her family. They graciously accepted and brought her back into their caring household. Oh, thank God for their love and understanding.

Her family (brothers) did that as a sign of acceptance and restoration to her rightful place in the family despite the evil the enemy had intended for her destruction. This bespeaks that irrespective of what may have transpired in your life, you too can be restored and strengthened to the newness of love and faith in God. You too have a brother in Jesus who can restore you, because God through Him is a restorer. In fact, His word is awash with examples of people who learned to return to Him and made things right.

Out of His great and incomparable love, God can restore anyone; it does not matter if it was sexual abuse, rape and so forth. And not only will He restore, but He will also cleanse and purify the person by the precious blood of Jesus. He will give them a new start and a new stand as though nothing ever happened to them. Dinah's brothers did that to her by taking her back from the jaws of the enemy. They did not question her as to why and how she ended up in Shechem's room. And God will not question you as to how and why such and such a thing happened to you. He is big enough to handle any situations you might find yourself in.

This does not mean He will condone your particular situations. But neither will He condemn you for whatever may have been done to you, or whatever you may have done yourself. Instead, He will forgive and cleanse you of the mess of such ill-timed sexual activities, if you truthfully seek Him. I don't want to make it sound like God does not care about bad things that happen to us, He does. Yet, He does not relate or deal with us based on such situations. If He did, none of us would stand any chance before Him.

You must have heard the story of the woman who was paraded, probably naked before Jesus. She was brought in, being pushed by men into one of Jesus' meetings. Those men claimed to have caught her red-handed in the very act of sexual involvement with a man not her husband. The situation was dire as everyone in the crowd was baying for her blood. To make matters even worse, their laws gave them express permission to kill such a woman by stoning.

Yet before they did that they thought it appropriate to seek Jesus' opinion first. And based on His love and compassion for people, in that case, the woman in question; Jesus prudently engaged the religious crowd and saved her life. He did not zero in on her supposed sin, but on how she could be restored to her personal dignity and worth and be made to love God. This to me is God's will for everybody; it does not matter their situations or conditions. If they desire and need restoration, God is always ready for them. Thus, I commend everyone to God's gracious dealings.

With that I encourage you to look at life widely, not only in terms of your bad experiences. Realize that you have a future, and generally the future is always brighter than the past. Indeed, your future can be fulfilling if you embrace God's grace. View yourself appropriately and shun youthful relationships that see things only in terms of youthful love and sex. At an appropriate time you will appreciate you waited. Of course, sacrificing to wait is sometimes difficult and even lonesome, but it is the best option as the results are always pleasant.

On the other hand, people who slip around playing with sex always live with regrets. They often carry the burden of wretched unclean living arising from their carnal curiosities.

Yet it is important here to note that there is help available out there for every situation; seek help as may be necessary in your particular case. Be bold and refuse to be held back by fear or shame. Sometimes it proves difficult for people to freely discuss their situations, but it is worth coming out if you are to be helped. There are organizations and groups of trusted counselors and experts out there, who deal with such situations daily. They have helped millions of people and they can help you rediscover sexual wholeness after being abused or misused.

You are not alone; others have also undergone similar situations and have come out even stronger than they would have expected. They then formed various support groups where you can join and find help. There is mutual support, encouragement and support necessary for your healing process in such groups. These are some of the places to go that can help with your recovery.

The solidarity in such groups is profound and cannot be found in standing alone. One of the biggest hindrances to recovery after such circumstances is keeping quiet, or trying to hide whatever happened to you. Do not go that route, you are not the first person to have suffered such an experience. There are millions of others out there; so come out clearly and let it be known that you have been a victim of such a horrific experience.

Like they say, when you join such a group you are joining *a family*; where professional help and heartfelt encouragement, in an environment of continuous understanding are very much available. When distressed and seemingly friendless, not knowing what to do or where to go; go to the *family*. You will be embraced and listened to with support and care unrivaled. That is where and when you can begin to find your healing.

In summary:

- Sexual abuse (in this case rape) can happen to anyone.
- If that happens, do not blame yourself. You did not invite the aggressor; they perpetrated it on you because of their own problems. Some of such people are sick.
- Manage your emotions properly if you happen to be a victim of rape or other forms of sexual abuses. This is important to help prevent your slipping off into self-pity and depression.
- Consider seeking professional help whenever possible, and get every necessary assistance as soon as possible.
- Learn as much as you can about healthy living after such traumatic experiences.
- Find support by joining a community of people with similar experiences.
- Be open for help wherever it may be found and keep your channels of communications open.

- Be wise, be informed and take nothing for granted. Do not presume that nothing bad can ever happen to you.

Even Dinah did not anticipate that such a bad thing could happen to her, but it did. Be careful and watch out for control freaks, especially young men who always want to control every aspect of their relationships with young women. Some of them become very possessive of the girls and make great demands upon them to the point of controlling even their very wardrobes and make-ups. It is unfortunate but true.

They have their own problems, and are known never to accept a no for an answer from girls or women. But you must not subject yourself to such mindless controllers. Enter into a relationship as an equal partner looking for relational capacity developments, and not just for sex.

John C Maxwell, a New York Times bestselling author says that one of the first rules in human relations is to seek common ground with others. . . Comparing similar experiences and discovering shared beliefs can pave way for successful relationships.[7] Thus, be hesitant in involving

---

[7]John C Maxwell, *Ethics 101: What Every Leader Needs To Know.* Center Street; 1st Center Street Ed edition (May 11, 2005)

with those whose main objective is simply sex. They will hurt you and dump you. They may even ruin your life!

Hence, don't throw caution to the wind and thereby destroy your future. Be hesitant over things you do not want, or things you are uncomfortable with. Take time and weigh out the implications of your every involvements. If you are not sure of some things, ask those adults in your life. Don't seek other youths' counsel in weighty matters. They don't have the necessary life experiences to advice you accordingly.

By observing this simple wisdom, you would be on your way to worthwhile living. Therefore, take a stand and be counted amongst those who love God enough to exemplify His reasonable, and respectful love. It is true; sexual fidelity has got its own temptations, but promiscuous lifestyle is worst as it has no blessings of peace and soundness. There are always every kinds of apprehensions with it.

Finally, be ready to learn and relearn even things you thought you already knew. Develop non-exploitative friendships, and continue to enjoy God's grace. Yet, you cannot do that adequately without having a personal commitment to, and a sound relationship with God. That's what we want to talk about shortly in the next chapter. Before then:

Some Questions to Ponder

1. As the story of Dinah comes to a close, I have related other case-situations involving other people. How come such situations keep occurring? Why do you think people don't seem to learn from others?
2. Why is it that some people, especially young men turn out to be controllers in their relationships? Are they suffering from some type of complex? Is it insecurity? Discuss
3. Some girls or young women get into relationships as a means of filling a void in their lives left by lack of a father, an absent father or father figure. Is that the cure for their circumstances? How would you advise them?
4. Why is it necessary for those who have had a traumatic or an abusive experience to join a community of persons who share their experiences? Explain.
5. Why should young people wait in matters of sexual involvements? Give reasons and examples if possible.

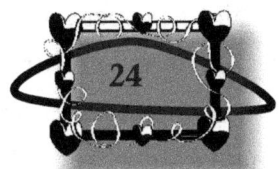

Relationship with God the Key

The relational expression we exhibit toward others are formed in the cradle of our families. That is, the way we relate with others arises out of our family conditioning. In his book *the Father Connection*[8]; Josh McDowell states that a child's relationship with Dad is a decisive factor in that young person's health, development and happiness. And there is a parallel with this when it comes to life in God. If we relate properly with God it will show in the way we treat others.

---

[8] Josh McDowell; The Father Connection: How You Can Make the Difference in Your Child's Self-Esteem and Sense of Purpose: B&H Books; Updated edition (May 1, 2008)

Nonetheless, there are those young people who either have no fathers present in their lives due to various reasons. Research has shown that father factor is very important in every child's proper social development. Yet in those situations where fathers are absent the young people need to embrace the fatherhood of God over their lives. He is the ultimate Father, and relationship with Him is the key to a wholesome life.

Thus, when our earthly dads are not available, or have let us down; we need to realize that we have a greater Father in God. He has promised never to leave us nor forsake us, and that accordingly boosts our life outlooks and sense of purpose making us secure in Him. Moreover, when we enter into a relationship with God; He brings us into a community of His people where fathers and other role model figures are readily available and can guide and mentor the young people accordingly. Young people should therefore identify and join such communities and they will find love and proper guidance for their lives.

Yet no one ever has an automatic relationship with God. It is something we must consciously enter into, otherwise we remain in our dysfunctional human natures that we inherited from Adam. That is why we hurt and abuse others, more so in sexual matters. We have a fallen nature that makes it difficult, if not impossible for us to live selflessly. Our desires are corrupted by that fallen nature, which mostly tends towards wrongdoing. We may not want to do evil, but we find ourselves doing it anyway. And this is reflected in every facet of our lives.

Especially, because of that corruption in our nature; we have particularly cheapened sex in our societies today. The society is obsessed with sex as the liberal culture redefines everything based on the opinions of the so-called experts. This has led to sexual perversions of every kind. Indeed, through the liberal media today: porn, sexting and phone-sex are exposed even to children. Sex has become a medium used to sell everything and is even depicted in cartoons. Its preciousness and importance has been eroded to the end. But how do we get out of this predicament? By appealing to God's grace; it is our way out.

> *For the grace of God has been revealed, bringing salvation to all people. And it instructs us to turn from godless living and sinful pleasures. That is, we should live in this evil world with wisdom, righteousness, and devotion to God*, declares the good book.

God's grace enables people to live godly in any circumstances, and it can empower us too to do so in this present world. More so young people should begin laying themselves a foundation of godliness even as early as now.

But they can do that only by embracing Yahweh's grace in entering into a personal relationship with Him. It is what brings salvation and infuses the recipient with His power to live righteously with devotion to Him. Why the moral breakdown in the society? Because people have neglected Yahweh's grace.

You could be reading this and you are living outside God's grace. If that is the case friend, then I urge you to consider experiencing Yahweh's grace on a personal level. How? By accepting His gift of eternal life in His Son, who brought grace and truth abundantly to us. It is recorded that in His Son God has given us eternal life, which we can partake of only by accepting that Son in the invitation to register ourselves with the Commonwealth of the redeemed.

This is in view of the unprecedented occasion of the reunion and celebration of His Son's unsurpassed accomplishment for human redemption. Everyone aspiring to be part of that celebration must welcome the Son into their life. The Son is the savior who out of great love gave His life for the world while the world was stooped in sin. Receiving Him is the only guarantee to have your name in the list of the redeemed.

If you are like me then your reaction should have been something like, "Oh where do I sign up my name"? That is a good question which deserves an answer. Yes, you are supposed to sign up your name with God. And people from all over the world and from all walks of life have been invited to do so. It is by invitation only to attend that wonderful ceremony of its kind. Nothing like it has been witnessed and neither shall there be. It will be held at the yet to be completed Emerald - Jasper City Square, with golden street and pearly gates.

The transportation arrangements too are already in place. It is understood they will use the grand hyper technology involving the beaming system (rapture) that far supersedes anything you might have watched in some of the Sci-fi movies. This will lift up people from every corner of the earth, even from the remotest regions provided they would have signed up for the ceremony.

And seating reservations are only by signed declaration of the willingness and commitment to attending. That is, by signing your name you are authorizing them to make your seating arrangements also. This may sound stranger than fiction, but it is true dear friend. The organizers of this great event have remarked that "…nothing unworthy will be allowed to enter. No one who is dirty-minded or who tells lies will be there. Only those whose names are written in *the Lamb's book of life* will be in the city."[9]

The Lamb's book of life is where your name must be signed in. I hope you are beginning to understand what I am talking about. It is the *Marriage Supper of the Lamb;* the culmination of the Divine love involving the humanity. God's love for humanity made Him take the frail human form upon Himself to come to our level to redeem us. With that, He brought reconciliation between the heavens and the lost humanity that had been at enmity with Him since Adam's rebellion and defection.

Yet, that enmity was not go on like that forever. It had to have an end somewhere by our taking the step of making peace with God. He says, "But as many as received Him, He gives power and the right to be called God's children. They are those who believe on His name".[10]

Anyone who receives Him, begins their *peace process* with Him and their names are automatically enrolled in the Lamb's book of life. This is very important to understand, because everyone who did not situate their names in that book missed the ceremony. They were all excluded by their lack of action.

This is why I urge everyone to make sure their names are signed in there. It is unfortunate that people

---

[9] Revelation 21:27
[10] John 1:12

walk the earth with their names literally everywhere: on their job, bank accounts, social media, doctor's records and so forth; yet missing from the Lamb's book of life.

Do not hesitate, make a wise decision to sign your name in the Lamb's book of life today. Simply acknowledge as part of the human race that you have fallen short of God's designed plan, which came about by Adam's sin in Eden when he obeyed Satan and despised God.

This means everyone who has not been reconciled to God from Adam's actions, is a stranger to the commonwealth of the redeemed and is still a sinner. They will not enter into that gathering. But God has provided for everyone's inclusion simply by their accepting His invitation and offer of life through His Son. That is the way to make peace with Him.

There are no other arrangements people need to make when it comes to this; God has done all there was to be done. He has made a way for all to come in and He made sure they can come right in through His gates of splendid grace, at any time. The gate into God's grace has not been shut and His arms are wide open.

The good Book intimates that God does not want anyone to miss out on that great day. He, indeed, desires that all should come to His Son, who averred that He will receive all who come to Him. He said, "Whosoever comes to me, I shall in no wise turn away." His invitation went out to all who are in turmoil and are burdened with life issues to go to Him and He would give them rest.

There is no time you can come to Him and find the "we are closed" sign. In God your arrival is always anticipated; He is always ready for you. There are no other arrangements you are to make, just come as you are and He takes it from there.

Sometimes you may even feel unworthy or that you are not ready. Yet that does not matter at all to God. Yours is simply to come to Him by faith and His grace will begin its effects in your heart. Jesus Himself stated as we observed above that whosoever comes to Him He will in no wise turn away. I can assure you friend, Jesus will never for any reason turn you away. His love for us is forever; a purifying agent that ushers us into His grace. Thereafter, that grace triggers the flow of His peace like a river into our hearts. It is what I refer to as making peace with God.

> "Therefore being justified by faith, we have peace with God through our Lord Jesus Christ."[11]

Another Translation reads:

Therefore, since we have been made right in God's sight by faith, we have peace with God because of what Jesus Christ our Lord has done for us.

There is no other known way of making peace with Him, but by faith in Jesus Christ. He is the one who declared Himself our life and the way to the Father. This is not talking about trying to be good, or registering your name in some religious organization somewhere. It is not even being water baptized or being religious. Those are human exercises that are meaningless in themselves. They must come after you have made peace with God. Thus, everyone must deal with and answer 'the peace' with God question first.

Have you personally made peace with God? This is not in anything you do apart from accepting God's offer of life for you.

---

[11] Romans 5:1

"But God commendeth his love toward us, in that, while we were yet sinners, Christ died for us."[12]

"And you that were sometimes alienated and enemies in your minds by wicked works, yet hath he reconciled."[13]

God's great love is perfectly satisfying and will change your life if you embrace it. It is what people are searching for the world over; even in relationships, in sex and so forth. In fact, it is what Shechem was looking for from Dinah.

But you can never find a lasting and totally fulfilling relationship from anyone else. Why? Because people are just as humans as yourself. They have their shortcomings and hang-ups, needs and fears. God alone can everlastingly and perfectly fulfill us. We have to individually respond to Him for this fulfillment, and then our other relationships will make sense. This is what it all boils down to, and I call it getting into the grace of God.

---

[12] Roman 5:8
[13] Colossians 1:21

That is, you personally have to respond to Him for His life. Others can tell you about it; they can pray for you, but in the final analysis you are the one who must individually respond and experience it. Indeed, faith in God is a personal experience that always change the course of people's lives and histories. I, therefore, urge you to give God a chance in your life today; get into His grace and make peace with Him. He will set you free and give you a right standing with Him. And it is the key to your other relationships.

You might want to do this but do not even know how. It is simple, just bow your head and open your heart to Him in a simple prayer like the following:

> Lord God I recognize my need of You. I have lived in ignorance of your love for me. Yet now I realize my folly and repent of my sinful lifestyle. I ask you to forgive me, and inscribe my name in your book of life as my enrolment to the Marriage Supper of the Lamb. I accept Jesus to be my Lord and savior now. I know He will make me a part of your family. Thank You for your offer of life through Him. Amen.

This is the best way to end this amazing story of Dinah Jacob by personally receiving God's life and friendship. Thanks for reading. Live wisely and wholly, and keep learning how to love appropriately and positively.

Some Questions to Ponder

1. What do you understand by the term right relationships? Can we attain such relationships so we do not hurt others?
2. From the start of this book almost to its end, there is one major recurring theme - betrayal. It began with Dinah's father betraying and defrauding his brother Esau of his birthright. There are many more in the book; can you identify and discuss them? What does this tell us about life in general?
3. Why does the author say relationship with God is the key to other relationships? Discuss
4. If you were to summarize the message of this book in a few words what would that be?